THE BLUEPRINT OF KARM

“DISCOVER THE SOLUTIONS YOU'VE BEEN SEARCHING FOR”

PRADYUMAN SHARRMA

Made with ♥ on the Notion Press Platform
www.notionpress.com

"Dedicated to my Maate, Pitashree, Nani and Sonal with all my love and gratitude, your unwavering guidance, support, and love have been the foundation of everything I do. This book is a reflection of the values you instilled in me. May the wisdom and teachings of our ancestors continue to guide us all?"

Contents

Foreword *vii*

Preface *ix*

Acknowledgements *xiii*

Prologue *xv*

1. Is Karm Known To Us? 1
2. The Many Shades Of Karm: Do We Have It Figured Out? 6
3. Breaking The Cycle Of Karm: Rewriting Your Destiny 14
4. The Role Of Dharm In Healing Karm 21
5. Dharm, Karm, And Goals 25
6. Karm And Relationships: Healing Through Understanding 30
7. Karm And Success: Aligning Action With Purpose 38
8. The Law Of Attraction And Karm: Manifesting With Purpose 45
9. Karm And Health: The Mind-Body Connection 52
10. Meditation And Mindfulness: Unlocking The Power Of The Present Moment 61
11. Surrender: The Art Of Letting Go And Trusting The Flow 69
12. The Importance Of Self-Love In Transforming Karm 77
13. Embracing Your Destiny: The Final Step Towards Spiritual Mastery 85

Contents

14. Karm And The Collective Karm Of Society 92

15. Living A Karmically Aligned Life: Daily Practices For Transformation 100

16. Karmic Healing Through Art And Creativity: A Holistic Approach To Transformation 109

17. The Divine Play Of Karm: Understanding The Bigger Picture 117

Trailer for the Next Edition: 123

Final Thoughts: A New Beginning 125

FOREWORD

It is with great honor that I write the foreword for Karm, a deep and insightful book by Pradyuman Sharrma. Having known him for years, I've witnessed his genuine curiosity and dedication to understanding life's intricacies, especially the concept of karma.

Karm is more than a philosophical exploration; it provides a practical framework for applying the timeless principles of karma to our everyday decisions and actions. Through his words, Pradyuman has given readers a pathway to live more purposefully, understanding that each action we take has both immediate and far-reaching consequences.

As this is his first book, I believe readers will appreciate the clarity and wisdom with which Pradyuman explains complex ideas, making them accessible and actionable. I encourage you to embark on this journey with an open mind, as Karm has the potential to inspire profound personal growth.

— Himanshu Joshi

Preface

In every moment of our lives, we are the architects of our own destinies. Each thought we think, each decision we make, and each action we take creates a ripple that shapes our present reality and influences our future. But what if the patterns of our lives—our relationships, our successes, our failures—are not purely random? What if they are the result of deeper, unseen forces, shaped by our past actions, thoughts, and experiences?

This book, The *Karm Blueprint: Solve your problems and rewrite your story* "Discover The Solutions You've Been Searching For", delves into one of the most profound and transformative concepts of ancient philosophy: **karm**. More than just a simple belief or religious principle, karm is a powerful law of the universe, governing the cause and effect that underlies all human experience. It is not something that happens to us, but something that **we create**. And while karm has often been seen as an inevitable force, this book aims to offer you a new perspective: **you can rewrite your karm**.

For too long, many of us have been stuck in patterns—repeating the same mistakes, attracting the same challenges, or finding ourselves trapped in unhealthy relationships. We wonder why we continue to face the same hurdles, despite our best efforts to change. The answer lies in the concept of karm: we are often bound by invisible threads woven from our past actions, thoughts, and choices. **But this book is a roadmap for freedom.**

Throughout these pages, you will discover how karm operates not only in the external world but also within our minds, hearts, and souls. You'll learn how unresolved emotional baggage, old habits, and ingrained patterns can keep us stuck in cycles that prevent growth and happiness. But more importantly, you'll gain practical tools to break free from these cycles, heal the wounds of the past, and create new, more empowering patterns that align with your true purpose.

Why this book?

This book is not just an exploration of the philosophical or spiritual aspects of karm, but a **practical guide to transforming your life**. It provides actionable steps and exercises to help you identify the hidden forces at play in your life, understand the root causes of recurring patterns, and implement powerful strategies to rewrite your destiny.

Each chapter offers real-life stories, spiritual wisdom, and mindfulness practices that will empower you to recognize when you are operating from old karmic patterns and shift to a more conscious, empowered way of living. This book will show you how to:

- **Understand the laws of karm** and how they shape your experiences.
- **Recognize patterns** that no longer serve you and break free from them.
- **Develop mindfulness** to stay present and choose actions that align with your higher self.
- **Transform your relationships**, career, and inner world by rewriting your emotional and mental narratives.
- **Manifest with purpose**, using the law of attraction in harmony with your soul's true purpose.

By the end of this book, you will have the tools to stop being a passive participant in your life and become an active creator of your own destiny.

A Journey of Transformation

We are all on a journey. Every experience, every challenge, every joy, and every sorrow is part of the greater story of our lives. But we often forget that we are the writers of our own stories. We have the power to revise, to reframe, and to rewrite the narrative at any given moment. This is the beauty and the power of karm: it is not a fixed set of rules, but a dynamic and fluid process that we can influence.

In The *Karm Blueprint: "Discover The Solutions You've Been Searching For"*, I invite you to explore this transformative potential. Whether you are seeking to heal from past hurts, transform your relationships, or manifest your deepest desires, the tools you'll find in these pages will help you step into a new chapter of your life—one that is filled with purpose, clarity, and empowerment.

This is more than a book about karm. It's a guide to becoming the best version of yourself, the version of yourself that aligns with your highest potential and your deepest truth. As you read through these chapters, take time to reflect, absorb, and apply the insights you gain. Trust that the changes you make today will create a brighter, more fulfilling tomorrow.

Are you ready to break free from the cycle and take control of your destiny?

Let's begin the journey of rewriting your karm, one conscious choice at a time.

With gratitude and hope for your transformation,

Pradyuman Sharrma

ACKNOWLEDGEMENTS

I would like to express my deepest gratitude to three remarkable individuals, **Mr. Himanshu Joshi, Mr. Sameer Patel and Mr. Pankaj Kumar Gupta** whose support, guidance, and encouragement have been invaluable throughout the creation of this book.

To Mr. Sameer Patel, thank you for inspiring me with your sharp intellect and spontaneous thinking. Your ability to view the world with fresh perspectives has taught me to embrace creativity and spontaneity in my own life. Your insights were pivotal in shaping the core ideas of this work, and I am profoundly grateful for your thoughtful contributions.

To Mr. Pankaj Kumar Gupta, your unwavering belief in the importance of spontaneous thought and action has been a driving force behind the development of this book. Your guidance pushed me to explore new dimensions of creativity, and your constant encouragement helped me break through limitations I had unknowingly set for myself.

To Mr. Himanshu Joshi, your insightful advice and steady support have been instrumental in the realization of this book. Your belief in my ability to bring my thoughts to life and your patient encouragement through each step of this journey have made a lasting impact. I am grateful for your perspective and for always being there with wisdom and positivity when I needed it most.

Together, all of you have played a central role in helping me think beyond the conventional and embrace the beauty of spontaneity in my work. Thank you for your unwavering support, for believing in me, and for always encouraging me to think freely and boldly.

This book stands as a testament to the power of thinking spontaneously, and I dedicate it to all of you.

Prologue

We are all writing our own stories, whether we are aware of it or not. Each moment, each decision, every thought, and every emotion is a thread woven into the intricate tapestry of our lives. Yet, too often we live as passive participants in our own narratives, reacting to circumstances rather than actively shaping them. We are not fully aware of the invisible forces at play, those subtle energies that influence our actions, our relationships, and the way we experience the world.

One of the most powerful of these forces is karm—the law of cause and effect, the invisible thread connecting every action to its consequence, every thought to its manifestation. Karm is not just a spiritual or philosophical concept; it is the blueprint for our life's unfolding. It shapes our experiences, governs the patterns that repeat in our relationships, careers, and personal growth, and, if left unchecked, keeps us cycling through the same struggles and challenges, again and again.

But what if we could change that? What if we could break free from these cycles, recognize the hidden patterns that no longer serve us, and rewrite the course of our lives with intention and purpose? This book is an invitation to do just that.

I

Is Karm Known to Us?

Introduction to Karm: What It Really Is

Karm is one of the most misunderstood concepts in modern spirituality and popular culture. Most people associate karm with a simple cause-and-effect relationship, often misinterpreted as "what goes around, comes around." While this view isn't entirely incorrect, it only scratches the surface of what karm truly is.

Karm is not just about the actions we take but also about the intentions behind them. It is the ongoing process that connects our thoughts, words, and deeds to the universe around us. The way we think and feel affects not only our own lives but also the lives of those around us.

But do we truly understand the nature of karm? Or are we simply following the surface-level understanding, relying on the idea of cosmic justice to explain life's difficulties?

Let's explore this through a deeper lens, starting with a story...

Ajay's Story: A Journey into Karm

Ajay was an ordinary man, a young professional living in Mumbai. Like many others, he had dreams, aspirations, and the desire to build a better future for himself. Ajay had heard of the term "karm" but only in passing. To him, it was simply about "good" and "bad" actions, and the belief that the universe would balance everything in the end. Little did he know, karm was about to teach him a far deeper lesson than he had imagined.

Ajay had always been drawn to the idea of quick success. He worked hard, but like many people, he was impatient. He dreamed of finding a shortcut to wealth and prosperity, just like his old friend Ravi, who had made a fortune through stock trading.

One day, Ajay met Ravi for coffee, and Ravi shared his success story—how he had turned a small investment into a huge profit by mastering options trading in the stock market. Ajay was fascinated. He immediately jumped into the world of trading, convinced that this was the key to his dreams.

The first few days were promising. Ajay made a small profit, which fed his excitement and ego. He felt he had discovered the secret to success. But the excitement quickly turned into greed. The more he traded, the more he felt compelled to chase bigger profits, even if it meant taking higher risks. He ignored the red flags and warning signs, driven by an obsessive need for more.

On day five, things went terribly wrong. Ajay lost a significant portion of his savings. His excitement turned to panic. He tried to make up for his losses by taking more risks, but things only got worse. His losses spiralled out of control, and soon he found himself in debt. What was once a hopeful venture had turned into a nightmare?

The Karm Behind the Story: Analysing Ajay's Actions

At first glance, it might seem like Ajay's story is a simple tale of someone who tried their luck and failed. But if we look deeper, we can see the intricate dance of karm at work.

Ajay's initial success was not the result of any special skill or luck. It was the result of his spontaneous actions. When he entered the market with a beginner's mind-set, his actions were driven by curiosity and instinct. However, once he started to focus solely on making more money, his decisions were governed by greed and the need for validation. These emotions blinded him to the risks and consequences of his actions.

Ajay's karmic journey was disrupted when he let non-spontaneous karm take over. Instead of acting in alignment with his true self and values, he allowed his ego and desires to control him. He believed that quick success was the goal and didn't realize that every action has a ripple effect. This was not just about the loss of money—it was about the loss of control, peace, and integrity.

Spontaneous vs. Non-Spontaneous Karm

- **Spontaneous Karm:** This is when we act without overthinking, in alignment with our deeper values. Actions flow naturally, and they often lead to harmonious outcomes.
- **Non-Spontaneous Karm:** This happens when we act out of fear, ego, or overanalyses. These actions are disconnected from our true purpose and often lead to conflict, regret, and negative consequences.

Ajay's fall from grace was the result of his non-spontaneous karm. By becoming obsessed with outcomes and ignoring the natural flow of life, he disrupted the balance and invited hardship.

The Real Lesson of Karm: Becoming Aware

The story of Ajay is not just a cautionary tale; it's a lesson in how our actions—whether spontaneous or nonspontaneous—shape our experiences. Karm is not just about good or bad deeds; it's about awareness. When we are aware of our motivations and the consequences of our actions, we can choose wisely and live in harmony with the world around us.

Reflection Exercise:

- **Journal Prompt:** Think of a time when you made a decision based on impulse or fear. What were the consequences? What do you wish you had done differently? Write down your thoughts on how spontaneous actions can lead to more fulfilling outcomes.

- **Mindfulness Practice:** For the next week, observe your actions closely. When you act spontaneously, notice how it feels. When you act out of fear or overthinking, notice the tension or discomfort. Write down your observations.

II

The Many Shades of Karm: Do We Have It Figured Out?

At first glance, the concept of karm might seem straightforward. The ancient law of cause and effect teaches us that every action, thought, and intention we engage in will inevitably bear fruit. This idea is simple, even intuitive. If you do good, good will come to you. If you harm others, harm will return to you. In its most basic form, karm can seem like a simple equation. But is it really that simple? Or is there much more to it than we have figured out?

As we dive deeper into the subject, we'll see that karm is not a one-size-fits-all law but a complex and nuanced force that governs not just the results of our actions, but the very fabric of our consciousness, our perceptions, and our reality. To truly understand karm, we need to explore its many shades, its different forms, and the subtle ways in which it shapes our lives. It's time to move beyond the simplistic view of karm and uncover its layers—so we can navigate life with greater awareness, clarity, and power.

The Simplicity of Karm: Cause and Effect

At its core, karm is the law of cause and effect. This is the basic premise: every action has a consequence. Every thought and every intention we hold sends ripples into the universe, shaping our experiences and future outcomes. The idea is simple—like a seed planted in the soil, our actions eventually yield results, whether positive or negative. In this sense, karm operates much like a natural law—just as gravity pulls us down, karm brings back to us the energy we put out into the world.

However, when we take a closer look, we begin to realize that the process isn't always as clear-cut as it might seem. For example, you might do something "good"—you might help someone in need, act out of kindness, or make a sacrifice—and yet not immediately experience positive results. In contrast, someone who acts with selfish intent might face immediate success or rewards. So, does karm really follow a clear and predictable pattern?

The law of cause and effect is the simplest entry point into understanding karm, but it doesn't fully explain the depth and complexity of how karm works in the real world. The timing of karm, the nature of its consequences, and the deeper influences of past lives and hidden desires create a rich web of karmic forces that we often don't understand.

The Many Layers of Karm: Moving Beyond Cause and Effect

Karm is much more than just a transaction of good and bad actions. As we explore its deeper layers, we discover that karm operates on multiple levels—mental, emotional, spiritual, and even collective. Our actions are not isolated; they are influenced by our thoughts, intentions, and unconscious patterns, which accumulate over lifetimes. This makes karm a dynamic process that is constantly unfolding and evolving.

In ancient spiritual texts like the Upanishads and the Bhagavad Gita, karm is described not as a simplistic exchange of actions and consequences but as a sophisticated and multifaceted law that governs our life experiences. The deeper spiritual understanding of karm expands its meaning to include not only the external effects of our actions but also the internal, psychological, and spiritual imprints they leave behind.

Karm and the Upanishads: A Journey of the Soul

The Upanishads, ancient spiritual texts central to Hindu philosophy, describe karm as part of a larger spiritual journey. In this context, karm is not simply a moral ledger where good deeds outweigh bad ones. Instead, it is linked to the soul's journey through the cycles of birth, death, and rebirth. Each action we take, each decision we make, creates samskaras—impressions or seeds—that shape our consciousness and guide the unfolding of our lives.

Karm, according to the Upanishads, is a force that weaves through multiple lifetimes. The karm we accumulate in one life follows us into the next, influencing the circumstances we are born into and the challenges we face. This process continues until the soul reaches moksha, or liberation, where the cycle of karm and reincarnation is broken. The goal is to purify the soul through conscious actions, self-awareness, and spiritual practices, so that we no longer accumulate harmful karm that keeps us trapped in the cycle of suffering and rebirth.

Karm and the Bhagavad Gita: Action Without Attachment

The Bhagavad Gita, one of the most widely read spiritual texts, offers a different yet complementary perspective on karm. In the Gita, Lord Sri krishn teaches Prince Arjun about the nature of dharm (righteous duty) and karm. One of the key messages Sri krishn imparts is the idea of acting without attachment to the results of our actions—a concept that is central to understanding akarm (non-action) and spontaneous karm.

Sri krishn advises Arjun to perform his duty as a warrior, but without the burden of attachment to victory or defeat. He tells Arjun that the results of his actions are not in his control; what matters is the purity of his intentions and the commitment to acting in alignment with his higher self, without concern for personal gain. This teaching introduces a powerful principle: acting without attachment allows us to break free from the cycle of karm and approach life with a sense of peace, knowing that we are simply performing our duty in the best way we can.

The Bhagavad Gita provides an essential key to understanding the more subtle aspects of karm: it's not just about the actions themselves but about the internal state of the actor. By focusing on the quality of our intentions and maintaining a sense of detachment from outcomes, we can transform our karmic patterns and act from a place of spiritual clarity.

The Many Types of Karm: Vikarm, Akarm, Prarabdha, and Sanchit

To fully grasp the complexity of karm, we must understand its various forms. Karm is not a one-size-fits-all principle; it manifests in different ways depending on the nature of our actions, thoughts, and desires. The four primary types of karm are vikarm, akarm, prarabdha, and sanchit. Each type represents a different aspect of how karm influences our lives and our spiritual evolution.

Vikarm: Actions That Disrupt the Natural Flow

Vikarm refers to actions that go against the natural flow of life, actions that cause harm, disrupt harmony, or violate the principles of dharm (righteousness). These are the actions that lead to negative consequences, not just for the individual but for others as well.

For example, Ajay might decide to engage in unethical business practices to maximize his profits. His actions, motivated by greed and the desire for personal gain, are classified as vikarm because they disrupt the natural order and create suffering for others. Vikarm, in its essence, reflects an imbalance in our relationship with the world and others.

While the consequences of vikarm are often immediate or visible, the deeper effects can ripple through our lives, creating long-lasting patterns of suffering. The remedy for vikarm lies in conscious self-awareness and a commitment to living in alignment with dharm, or the natural law.

Akarm: The Freedom of Non-Attachment

On the other end of the spectrum lies akarm, the concept of "non-action." Akarm is not about doing nothing; rather, it refers to actions that arise from a state of deep alignment with the universe. In this state, actions are performed without attachment to results or ego-driven motives.

Sri krishn's teachings in the Bhagavad Gita emphasize the importance of performing actions without attachment. This practice is rooted in spontaneous karm, where our actions flow naturally from a place of love, compassion, and pure intention. When we act from this space, there is no expectation of reward, no desire to control the outcome, and no ego involved. The result is a life of peace, freedom, and alignment with our true self.

Prarabdha: The Karm We Are Currently Experiencing

Prarabdha is the karm that we have accumulated in past lifetimes (and in this lifetime) that is currently unfolding. These are the circumstances, challenges, and experiences we are facing right now. Prarabdha is the result of past actions that have come to fruition in the present.

For instance, if someone is born into a family with financial difficulties, this may be a result of their prarabdha—the karmic consequences of their past actions. However, it's important to note that while prarabdha shapes our present circumstances, it is not an unchangeable fate. Through conscious action, we can mitigate the effects of prarabdha and even transform our circumstances over time.

Sanchit Karm: The Storehouse of Past Actions

Finally, sanchit karm refers to the vast accumulation of karm from all our past lives. This is the "storehouse" of karmic impressions (samskaras) that influence our current life. While we cannot directly change sanchit karm, we can influence how it manifests in our lives by cultivating awareness and taking conscious action in the present.

Sanchit karm contains both positive and negative impressions. Our present life may reveal glimpses of sanchit karm through desires, fears, and tendencies that we are unaware of. By purifying the mind and spirit through conscious practices such as meditation, self-reflection, and compassionate living, we can begin to heal and transform these stored impressions.

Spontaneous Karm vs. Non-Spontaneous Karm:

Real-World Examples

Understanding spontaneous karm and non-spontaneous karm provides further insight into the ways karm manifests in our daily lives.

Spontaneous Karm: The Power of Unconscious Action

Spontaneous karm occurs when we act in alignment with our highest self, with love and compassion, without any conscious desire for reward. This is the kind of karm that flows naturally, like a river, without resistance or calculation.

For example, a mother may help a child in need without thinking twice, motivated purely by love. This act, while seemingly small, creates a ripple of positive energy that can transform not only the mother's life but the life of the child and others around them. It's a simple yet powerful example of spontaneous karm at work.

Non-Spontaneous Karm: Actions Driven by Ego and Attachment

In contrast, non-spontaneous karm arises when our actions are driven by fear, attachment, or a desire for control. These actions tend to create tension, stress, and negative consequences, because they are based on our ego's desire for outcomes.

Consider the example of a businessman who acts primarily out of fear of failure. His decisions are often calculated based on the risk of loss, rather than from a place of clarity or higher purpose. Over time, this creates stress, burnout, and strained relationships. His karm is dictated by fear, and it manifests as negative consequences in his life.

III

Breaking the Cycle of Karm: Rewriting Your Destiny

Introduction: Understanding the Karmic Cycle

At the heart of human experience lies a pattern—a cycle that repeats itself over and over again. Whether we realize it or not, many of us are caught in this cycle, repeating the same mistakes, facing similar challenges, or attracting the same kinds of relationships. This cycle is what we refer to as Karm.

In Eastern philosophy, particularly in Hinduism and Buddhism, karm is not merely a set of isolated actions but a force that shapes our present and future. The concept of samsara, or the cycle of birth, death, and rebirth, closely parallels the cyclical nature of karm. Every thought, word, and deed creates ripples in our consciousness, setting off a series of events that affect our present lives and the lives of those around us.

To truly break free from this cycle, we must first acknowledge that we are repeating patterns that stem from past actions, unresolved emotions, and deeply ingrained habits. This chapter delves into how these cycles form and, most importantly, how we can rewrite our destiny by breaking free from these cycles of karm.

The Karmic Cycle: Why We Repeat Our Mistakes

In order to break the karmic cycle, we first need to explore why we fall into the same patterns over and over again. To do so, let's look at the nature of karm more closely. Karm can be understood as a web of cause and effect that extends beyond this life and echoes in future ones. This web binds us to certain emotional, psychological, and behavioural patterns that shape our experiences.

Take the example of Neha, who repeatedly found herself in emotionally distant relationships. At first, she couldn't understand why she always seemed to attract the same type of person—someone who was emotionally unavailable or not fully invested in the relationship. Despite her best efforts to avoid the mistakes of the past, Neha would end up feeling lonely, frustrated, and stuck. This pattern persisted until she began exploring the roots of her behaviour.

As she reflected on her past, Neha realized that the issue went back to her childhood. Her parents, though loving, had a distant relationship. Her father, who was emotionally unavailable, often withheld affection, and her mother withdrew into herself when conflicts arose. As a child, Neha had absorbed this behaviour, and it became part of her inner world. In her adult relationships, she unconsciously mimicked this pattern of emotional detachment, pushing others away whenever she felt overwhelmed.

Neha's case demonstrates a fundamental truth: karm doesn't just exist in the external world—it operates within our inner landscape. The emotional patterns, attitudes, and beliefs we inherit, consciously or unconsciously, shape how we interact with the world. The unresolved emotional baggage from our past often manifests as a repeating karmic pattern, influencing the choices we make in the present.

How Karm Forms Patterns

To break the karmic cycle, we need to understand how it forms. Karm is not just a collection of random actions; rather, it is shaped by our mental and emotional patterns, also known as samskaras. These are the impressions left in our consciousness from past experiences that dictate how we perceive and react to the world.

Samskaras are the roots of our karm. They arise from our experiences and form habitual mental and emotional tendencies. These tendencies then guide our actions. For example, if you've had a traumatic experience in childhood that involved a betrayal, you may carry an unconscious belief that people are untrustworthy. This belief could shape your interactions with others and cause you to be suspicious or avoidant in relationships, even when there is no actual threat.

Breaking the cycle requires us to confront these samskaras head-on. We must recognize how our past experiences—particularly unresolved emotional wounds—are shaping our current reality. By doing so, we create an opportunity for healing and transformation. It's important to understand that this process is not about eliminating karm altogether, but about evolving it—transmuting the negative aspects of our past into sources of growth and wisdom.

Breaking the Cycle: Mindfulness and Self-Awareness

The most crucial step in breaking free from the karmic cycle is awareness. Without awareness, we remain blind to the forces driving our behaviour. It's easy to fall into the trap of blaming external circumstances or other people for the challenges we face. However, when we begin to practice mindfulness, we can start to recognize the internal patterns and triggers that lead us to repeat our mistakes.

Mindfulness is the practice of being fully present in the moment and observing our thoughts, emotions, and actions without judgment. By applying mindfulness to our everyday experiences, we create space between stimulus and response, allowing us to break free from the automatic patterns that keep us stuck.

Neha, for example, began to practice mindfulness during her interactions in relationships. She learned to pause and observe when she felt the urge to withdraw emotionally. Instead of reacting impulsively, she took a step back and reflected on why she felt the need to distance herself. This awareness helped her recognize that her fear of vulnerability was rooted in past experiences.

By consciously choosing to engage differently, Neha was able to rewrite her relationship karm. Instead of withdrawing, she communicated openly and worked through her fears. Mindfulness allowed her to shift her response to old triggers, thereby breaking free from the cycle of emotional detachment.

Real-Life Example: A Breakthrough Moment

The story of Raj, a young professional, offers another example of breaking free from karmic cycles. Raj had always struggled with procrastination. No matter how much he tried to overcome it, he would find himself putting off important tasks, especially at work. This pattern was frustrating, as he knew he was capable of achieving more, yet he couldn't shake the habit.

Through reflection, Raj realized that his procrastination was rooted in an intense fear of failure. Growing up, his parents had placed high academic expectations on him, often criticizing him for not meeting their standards. This created a sense of inadequacy that followed him into adulthood. The fear of not being good enough led him to procrastinate, as avoiding tasks allowed him to escape the possibility of failure.

Once Raj became aware of this deep-rooted fear, he began taking small, conscious steps to confront it. Rather than avoiding tasks, he started breaking his work into manageable pieces, allowing him to tackle each one without the overwhelming fear of failure. He also practiced self-compassion, allowing himself to make mistakes without harsh judgment. In doing so, Raj was able to reprogram his habitual response to fear and rewrite the karm of procrastination that had held him back for so long.

Tools for Breaking the Karmic Cycle

To break the cycle of karm, we need practical tools that help us become more conscious of our patterns and shift them. Here are several approaches that can aid in this transformation:

Mindful Action

The first step in changing any pattern is becoming aware of your habitual thoughts and behaviours. This requires mindfulness. Pay attention to your emotional and mental states before you take action. Are you acting out of fear, anger, or past hurt? Notice these feelings, and instead of reacting impulsively, choose to align your actions with your core values.

Forgiveness: Letting Go of the Past

Breaking free from the karmic cycle also requires forgiveness. Holding onto anger, resentment, or guilt keeps us tethered to the past. By practicing forgiveness—both of ourselves and others—we release the karmic charge that binds us to negative patterns.

Forgiveness doesn't mean condoning harmful actions; it means choosing to let go of the emotional weight associated with them. It means freeing ourselves from the past so that we can create a new future.

Rewriting the Narrative

The most powerful tool in breaking the karmic cycle is rewriting your personal narrative. Ask yourself, "What would my life look like if I were free from the patterns that have held me back?" Imagine how you would respond to a similar situation in the future. Write a new script for your life and begin to act in alignment with the person you want to become.

Reflection Exercise: Breaking Your Patterns

Pattern Identification

Think about a recurring pattern in your life—whether it's in relationships, work, or personal behaviour. Write down the following:

- When did you first notice this pattern?
- What triggers this behaviour?
- How has this pattern shaped your life?

Rewrite Your Karm

Now, imagine that you have the power to rewrite this pattern. How would you respond differently if you were free of the old tendencies? Write out a new course of action that aligns with your higher self and values. Make a commitment to take at least one step towards breaking this pattern in the coming week.

Conclusion

Breaking the cycle of karm is not an overnight process, but it is entirely possible. By cultivating awareness, practicing mindfulness, and rewriting our patterns, we can transform the habitual actions that have held us captive. Each moment offers us the opportunity to make a new choice, to shift our response, and to change the course of our destiny.

The cycle of karm is not an unbreakable chain; it is a series of lessons waiting to be learned. When we approach our patterns with love, compassion, and self-awareness, we empower ourselves to rewrite the story of our lives. In doing so, we transcend the cycles of the past and create a future that is aligned with our highest potential.

IV

The Role of Dharm in Healing Karm

What is Dharm?

In simple terms, Dharm refers to your life's purpose or your moral and ethical duty. In the context of karm, Dharm provides the blueprint for how we should live our lives in alignment with universal law. While karm deals with the consequences of our actions, Dharm offers us guidance on what actions are in harmony with the cosmic order.

In the Bhagavad Gita, Lord Krishna explains that performing one's Dharm leads to liberation (moksha). This means that when we act according to our true nature and higher purpose, we are able to transcend the cycle of karm.

The Connection between Dharm and Karm

The concept of Dharm can be understood as a guide for creating positive karm. When we live our lives in accordance with our Dharm, we are naturally aligned with universal principles. This alignment creates harmonious outcomes, allowing us to experience greater peace, fulfilment, and personal growth.

Let's return to the example of Neha. After realizing that her past patterns of emotional detachment were tied to unresolved karm, she also recognized that she had been ignoring her Dharm—the need to live with compassion and emotional openness. Neha's Dharm wasn't just about being successful in her career; it was about cultivating healthy, loving relationships that were built on trust, communication, and vulnerability.

By honouring her Dharm of openness and emotional authenticity, Neha was able to heal the wounds of her past and create a new kind of relationship dynamic—one based on mutual respect and understanding.

Dharm in Action: Real-Life Examples

1. **The Story of Arjun:** In the Bhagavad Gita, Arjun is faced with a moral dilemma on the battlefield of Kurukshetr. He is hesitant to fight against his own family members, but Krishna advises him to fulfil his Dharm as a warrior. Arjun's Dharm in this situation is to fight for justice and righteousness, even though it causes him personal pain. Arjun's internal struggle is a reflection of the tension between personal desires and the larger cosmic duty (Dharm).
2. **The Story of a Doctor:** Dr. Sita is a family physician who practices with integrity and compassion. Her Dharm as

a doctor is to heal others and alleviate their suffering, but this Dharm is not limited to her professional life. In her personal life, her Dharm is to be a loving wife, a nurturing mother, and a responsible member of her community. By aligning her actions with these duties, she cultivates positive karm that enriches her life and the lives of those around her.

How to Live in Alignment with Dharm

1. **Know Your True Purpose:** To live in alignment with your Dharm, you must first know who you are and what you are meant to do in this lifetime. This requires deep self-reflection and introspection. Spend time contemplating what brings you joy, what excites you, and what you feel called to contribute to the world.
2. **Act with Integrity:** Living according to your Dharm means making choices that honour your highest values. Whether you are at work, in a relationship, or in any other area of life, make decisions that are in line with your higher purpose.
3. **Serve Others:** Dharm is not just about self-fulfilment; it is about serving the greater good. Find ways to serve others—whether through your profession, your family, or your community. When we act selflessly and with compassion, we generate positive karm that leads to greater fulfilment and spiritual growth.

Reflection Exercise:

- **Discovering Your Dharm:** Take some time to reflect on your life's purpose. What do you feel most called to do? What roles do you play in your family, work, and community? How can you align your actions with these roles to fulfil your Dharm more fully?
- **Dharm in Daily Life:** Identify one area of your life where you can bring more integrity, service, or compassion. Write down specific actions you can take this week to honour your Dharm in that area.

V

Dharm, Karm, and Goals

The pursuit of goals is at the heart of most human endeavours. Whether it's achieving career success, building relationships, or seeking personal fulfilment, we set goals to guide our journey. But what role does Dharm play in this process? How does it shape our karm and ultimately influence the achievement of our goals?

The Essence of Dharm

Dharm is our inner compass, guiding us towards our true purpose. It's the path of righteousness that aligns our actions with our highest values. When we walk the path of Dharm, we feel a deep sense of fulfilment and alignment with our authentic selves. Dharm is what helps us prioritise what truly matters, whether it's kindness, honesty, or integrity. It's the thread that connects our values with our actions, ensuring that every step we take is in harmony with who we are meant to be.

Without Dharm, our goals can become misaligned, leading us astray. For example, a person might set a goal to become rich, but if they pursue this goal by exploiting others, using deceit, or engaging in morally corrupt behaviour, they are not acting in alignment with their Dharm. True success, therefore, comes from aligning our goals with Dharm. This alignment ensures that our pursuits bring not only material success but also inner peace and a sense of purpose.

Illustrative Story: The Student and the Competitive Exam

Consider the example of a student preparing for a competitive exam. This student has a goal—to secure a good job, build a stable future, and contribute positively to society. However, the path to that goal requires discipline, hard work, and integrity. If the student approaches their studies with honesty, dedication, and a sense of responsibility, they are acting in accordance with their Dharm. Their actions are aligned with their true purpose, and they experience a sense of peace because they know that they are doing what is right.

But if they resort to cheating, procrastination, or giving in to distractions, they are straying from the path of Dharm. Instead of focusing on righteousness, they are caught up in adharm—unrighteous actions that lead them away from their true purpose. The pursuit of the goal, even though it might bring temporary success, will never lead to long-term fulfilment because it is not aligned with the student's Dharm.

Aligning Goals with Dharm

True success lies in aligning our goals with Dharm. Whether it's a personal goal like learning a new skill, a career goal like securing a promotion, or a societal goal like making a positive impact on the world, every action we take towards achieving it should be in harmony with our values.

When our actions are aligned with Dharm, the universe responds in ways that support our journey. Karm, the law of cause and effect, plays a critical role here. Every action, thought, and intention we put forth creates ripples in the universe that eventually return to us. When we act in accordance with Dharm, our karm, both good and bad, are shaped by the integrity with which we pursue our goals. The journey towards our goal becomes less about the destination and more about the values we embody along the way.

Karm and the Path to Fulfilment

As we pursue our goals, we inevitably accumulate karm. If we pursue our goals with integrity, honesty, and compassion, the karm we create will be positive, leading to greater fulfilment and success. On the other hand, if we pursue our goals through manipulation, deceit, or self-centred motives, the karm we create will be negative, leading to dissatisfaction and obstacles.

Think of karm as the energy we send into the world. If we send out positive energy through righteous actions (Dharm), we will receive positive returns. If we send out negative energy through actions that are misaligned with our true values, we will face the consequences of those actions in the form of negative karm.

Individual Dharm vs. Social Dharm

While individual Dharm focuses on personal integrity, social Dharm is about our responsibilities to others. A person rooted in individual Dharm is more likely to contribute positively to society, fostering a sense of community and interconnectedness. However, both individual and social Dharm must be in balance for a fulfilling life.

Illustrative Story: The Corporate Leader and Social Responsibility

Take the example of a corporate leader who has set a goal to build a successful company. If this leader only focuses on personal success and neglects the welfare of their employees, the community, and the environment, their goal will be misaligned with social Dharm. True success comes from balancing personal ambition with a sense of responsibility towards others.

The leader may strive to increase profits and expand the business, but if they do so at the cost of employee well-being, ethical practices, or environmental sustainability, they are deviating from social Dharm. On the other hand, a leader who integrates Dharm into their leadership style—by creating fair wages, maintaining ethical practices, and giving back to the community—will not only achieve financial success but will also experience a deeper sense of fulfilment and impact.

The Role of Karm in Achieving Goals

Karm plays a crucial role in how our goals unfold. The intentions behind our actions, the way we treat others, and the choices we make all create ripples that affect the outcomes of our goals. Positive actions, guided by Dharm, lead to positive outcomes, while actions driven by selfish motives or unethical behaviour will lead to negative consequences.

For example, if a person sets a goal to become a successful entrepreneur, but they do so by exploiting others or acting dishonestly, they may achieve financial success in the short term. However, the negative karm generated from these actions will eventually lead to difficulties, challenges, and even failure. On the other hand, an entrepreneur who approaches their business with integrity, fairness, and compassion will not only achieve financial success but will also experience long-term satisfaction and growth.

Conclusion

The pursuit of goals is deeply intertwined with the concepts of Dharm and karm. By aligning our goals with Dharm, we ensure that our actions are in harmony with our values and purpose. This alignment helps us create positive karm, leading to a more fulfilling and meaningful life.

As we move forward in life, it is important to remember that our goals are not just about personal success. True fulfilment comes from contributing to the well-being of others and the world around us. By balancing individual Dharm with social responsibility, we can create a harmonious path to success, both for ourselves and for society.

VI

Karm and Relationships: Healing Through Understanding

Introduction: The Interconnectedness of All Beings

Relationships form the fabric of our daily lives. Whether familial, romantic, platonic, or professional, each relationship we have shapes us in some way. But what if these connections were more than mere social bonds? What if every relationship we experience, positive or negative, is a manifestation of karm? In the vast web of existence, our interactions with others reflect our past actions, desires, and spiritual lessons. Through the lens of karm, we come to realize that relationships are not just happenstance, but part of a deeper cosmic design.

This chapter explores the profound impact that relationships have on our karmic journey. By understanding how karm plays a role in every interaction, we gain insight into the reasons behind our connections—and how to cultivate healthier, more fulfilling relationships in the future.

What Are Karmic Relationships?

A karmic relationship is one that arises from the past—whether from previous lifetimes or earlier experiences in this one. These relationships are not merely coincidental; they are purposeful and deeply rooted in our spiritual growth.

Karmic bonds are formed when there is unfinished business from a past life or unresolved emotional, spiritual, or psychological issues. For example, we may encounter someone with whom we share a deep sense of familiarity or attraction, even if we've never met them before. This feeling often signifies that the relationship has a karmic undertone—a lesson or resolution that must be worked through.

Example

Karmic Relationships in Past Lives

Take the example of two souls who were once enemies in a past life. Perhaps they fought over the same territory or betrayed each other over matters of power. In their next life, they may be born into different circumstances, but still, they feel an inexplicable tension when they meet. This could manifest as an argument, jealousy, or even a deeper, more personal connection, but it is a karmic bond that they must resolve before they can move on.

Similarly, karmic relationships can also manifest in the form of unconditional love, where two souls are drawn together because they shared deep love or friendship in past lives. These relationships are marked by an overwhelming sense of familiarity, peace, and mutual respect.

Understanding Karmic Debt in Relationships

Every karmic relationship comes with an inherent karmic debt. If in the past we wronged someone, or failed to fulfil our duties toward them, we might encounter them in this life to rectify that imbalance. Similarly, if someone has wronged us, we may be presented with the opportunity to forgive them, heal, or face the consequences of their actions.

A karmic debt is the spiritual responsibility to resolve unfinished business—whether it be through forgiveness, learning, or transformation. Recognizing these debts allows us to heal and grow spiritually.

How Karm Affects Different Types of Relationships

Karm doesn't discriminate by relationship type. It permeates all kinds of interactions, from familial to romantic, friendships to professional relationships. However, the way karm manifests in each type of relationship can vary significantly.

Family and Ancestral Karm

Family is often the first environment where we experience karmic relationships. Ancestral karm plays a key role in the dynamics between generations. This can include unresolved family issues, inherited patterns of behaviour, or unhealed wounds passed down through the lineage.

Generational Karm and Patterns

For example, a child may be born into a family where addiction, financial struggles, or abuse are prevalent. The child, without understanding why, might be drawn into similar patterns, even if they consciously reject them. This indicates a karmic bond with their ancestors—perhaps from a past life where they were deeply involved in the same struggles.

Recognizing family karm requires introspection and understanding that we are often born into specific family systems for spiritual purposes. By healing and changing negative patterns, we not only heal ourselves but can also break the cycle for future generations.

Romantic Relationships and Soul mates

Romantic relationships are perhaps the most intense and challenging karmic bonds. Many people believe in the idea of soul mates—individuals who are meant to be together to fulfil a higher purpose. However, soul mates are not always synonymous with easy relationships. While they can bring joy and fulfilment, they can also highlight our greatest challenges.

Love and Pain: The Dual Nature of Karmic Love

A romantic relationship may bring immense love, but it can also expose unresolved wounds from the past, such as betrayal, abandonment, or insecurity. The pain we experience in such relationships is often a reflection of karmic lessons we need to learn.

For instance, if someone is unable to trust their partner despite the relationship being healthy, this could indicate unresolved trust issues from a past life. In such cases, the relationship serves as a mirror, showing us where we need healing.

Example: A Toxic Relationship as a Karmic Lesson

Imagine a person who repeatedly ends up in toxic relationships where they feel emotionally manipulated or neglected. In previous lifetimes, they might have been the perpetrator of such behaviour, and the karmic lesson now is to experience the opposite role—learning empathy, self-respect, and emotional intelligence.

These karmic dynamics in romantic relationships can be incredibly painful, but they also offer a deep opportunity for growth and healing.

Friendships: Spiritual Mirrors

Friendships can often serve as mirrors of our own self-worth, emotional needs, and unresolved issues. People we choose to be friends with may reflect qualities we are trying to develop or may expose areas where we have imbalances in our own lives.

The Spiritual Role of Friendships

Friendships are not merely for companionship—they also serve as spiritual teachers. A friend may challenge us to grow in certain areas, such as patience, trust, or forgiveness. In this way, friendships can be as karmic as romantic relationships or family dynamics.

For example, if we are constantly drawn to friendships where there is a power struggle, we may be holding onto past life issues related to competition or control. By recognizing these patterns, we can transform the relationship and evolve spiritually.

Professional Relationships: The Role of Karm in Workplaces

Workplace dynamics are often deeply karmic. The colleagues and superiors we encounter are likely part of our karmic cycle, giving us opportunities to learn patience, leadership, and collaboration.

Karm in Work Conflicts

If we find ourselves constantly clashing with a particular colleague or boss, it could indicate unresolved karmic issues related to authority or self-worth. The conflict may reflect something we need to heal within ourselves—be it pride, insecurity, or the need for control.

However, professional relationships also offer opportunities for service and selfless action. By working in alignment with our Dharm and maintaining integrity, we can transform even the most challenging professional interactions into spiritual lessons.

Healing Karmic Relationships

The ultimate goal in understanding karmic relationships is to heal and transform them, breaking free from negative patterns and moving toward spiritual growth.

- **The Power of Forgiveness in Karmic Healing**

Forgiveness is one of the most powerful tools in healing karmic relationships. Whether we are forgiving ourselves or others, releasing the grip of past hurts allows us to move forward with clarity and peace.

- **Forgiveness as a Release of Negative Karm**

In situations where we've been wronged by others, holding onto anger or resentment creates negative karm, which only perpetuates the cycle of pain. By practising forgiveness, we release the negative energy attached to the situation and open ourselves to healing.

- **The Role of Compassion and Empathy**

Cultivating compassion allows us to see others through the eyes of understanding, rather than judgement. When we develop empathy, we can understand the reasons behind others' actions, and we begin to break the cycle of karmic retribution.

- **Reflection and Self-Awareness**

Becoming aware of the karmic patterns in our relationships allows us to stop repeating the same mistakes. By reflecting on our past actions and recognizing where we've gone wrong, we can make conscious changes that alter the trajectory of our future.

Exercises for Healing Karmic Relationships

1. Journaling for Clarity

Take some time to reflect on your most significant relationships. Write down any patterns you've noticed in these relationships—both positive and negative. Are there recurring themes of conflict, trust issues, or unhealed wounds? Write about the lessons these relationships are trying to teach you.

2. Meditation for Forgiveness

Sit in a comfortable position and close your eyes. Visualize someone with whom you've had a challenging relationship. Focus on the pain or resentment you feel towards them. Then, with each breath, silently repeat the words: "I forgive you. I release you. I am free." Allow the energy of forgiveness to wash over you.

3. The Mirror Exercise

For a week, make a conscious effort to recognize the ways your relationships reflect aspects of your own character. Write down moments where you saw a piece of yourself reflected in someone else's behaviour. This exercise will help you identify karmic patterns and gain self-awareness.

Conclusion

Every relationship we have is an opportunity to grow spiritually. Whether it is a bond built on love or one marked by conflict, karmic relationships are part of our soul's journey. By understanding the karmic nature of these relationships, we can break free from destructive patterns and align our interactions with compassion, understanding, and forgiveness. The true power of relationships lies in their ability to shape us into better, more enlightened versions of ourselves.

VII

Karm and Success: Aligning Action with Purpose

In the modern world, the word "success" is often associated with material achievements. Financial wealth, career status, social recognition, and fame are frequently considered the ultimate indicators of success. Yet, in many spiritual traditions and philosophies, true success is not measured by these external markers. Rather, it is about living in alignment with one's inner values, fulfilling one's dharm (life purpose), and cultivating a deep sense of contentment and peace.

In this chapter, we will explore how success can be understood from a spiritual lens, emphasizing the importance of aligning one's actions with purpose, integrity, and a sense of duty to the greater good. We will also examine how the law of karm plays a central role in shaping our success—not merely as a passive principle but as an active and empowering force in achieving a meaningful and lasting form of prosperity.

Redefining Success: Material vs. Spiritual Fulfillment

Success in contemporary society is often reduced to material accomplishments. From a young age, many are taught to strive for wealth, power, recognition, and personal success as the ultimate goals of life. However, such a view of success tends to overlook the inner dimensions of fulfillment and well-being.

From a spiritual perspective, the true meaning of success cannot be determined solely by the accumulation of material wealth or status. These external achievements are transient and impermanent. They come and go, and while they may provide temporary satisfaction, they do not offer lasting happiness or contentment.

True success, therefore, is found in living authentically and in alignment with one's deeper purpose. It is about cultivating inner peace, integrity, and compassion. It is about contributing to the well-being of others and the greater good, while maintaining a strong connection to one's own values and spiritual path.

The Role of dharm in Achieving True Success

At the core of spiritual success is the concept of dharm—one's duty or life purpose. dharm refers to the unique path that each individual must walk, based on their values, talents, and inner calling. When we align our actions with our dharm, we experience a sense of fulfillment and joy that transcends material success.

Success, in this context, is not about what we achieve for ourselves alone, but about how we contribute to the world. It is about understanding that our actions have consequences and that we must act in a way that respects and nurtures both our own well-being and the well-being of others. This broader, more inclusive definition of success invites us to consider the impact we have on the world around us and to strive for balance, harmony, and alignment in everything we do.

Karm and the Pursuit of Material Success

One of the key concepts that underpin the spiritual view of success is karm, the law of cause and effect. In its simplest form, karm teaches us that the actions we take—both positive and negative—shape our future experiences. What we put out into the world, whether in thought, word, or deed, will eventually return to us in one form or another.

The connection between karm and material success can be understood through the example of Dev, an entrepreneur who initially pursued wealth and recognition above all else. At first, Dev's business flourished, and his material success grew. But despite the outward signs of achievement, he felt a growing sense of emptiness. His relationships were strained, his health declined, and he found himself constantly anxious and dissatisfied.

Through deep reflection and spiritual practice, Dev began to see that his relentless pursuit of success had been driven by a deep-seated insecurity. He was chasing external validation to fill an internal void. He realized that his actions—while successful in a worldly sense—had been motivated by ego and fear, rather than by a genuine desire to contribute to the greater good.

By realigning his intentions and actions with his deeper values, Dev shifted his focus from mere financial success to building a company that could serve a higher purpose. He started creating products that contributed positively to society, focusing on ethical business practices, and prioritizing the well-being of his employees and customers. As he did this, Dev found a new sense of peace and fulfillment. His business continued to thrive, but now, it was fueled by a sense of purpose rather than ego-driven ambition. His material success, though still present, was now secondary to the fulfillment he found in living authentically.

Aligning Action with Purpose: The Path to True Fulfillment

The key takeaway from Dev's story is that success comes when we align our actions with our deeper purpose. True success is not about the pursuit of wealth or recognition alone; it is about acting with integrity, staying true to our values, and serving a greater purpose. When we operate from a place of inner alignment, our actions become more meaningful, and the results of those actions are more likely to be aligned with our true desires.

The Importance of Intentionality

To align action with purpose, it is essential to act with intentionality. This means approaching each task with awareness and mindfulness, fully understanding why we are doing what we are doing. When we act with intention, we are not merely going through the motions or reacting to external pressures; instead, we are consciously choosing how to act based on our values and long-term goals.

Intentional action is especially important when it comes to our work and professional lives. In the workplace, it is easy to become caught up in the rat race, chasing promotions, bonuses, and recognition. However, when we approach our work with a sense of purpose and a commitment to serving others, we shift our focus from competition to collaboration, from ego to service. This shift in mindset allows us to create deeper, more meaningful connections with colleagues, clients, and customers. It also opens the door to greater personal fulfillment, as we begin to see our work as an extension of our values and beliefs.

Practical Steps for Aligning karm with Success

Now that we understand the principles of dharm, karm, and intentionality, let's look at some practical steps you can take to align your actions with your higher purpose and create lasting success:

1. Clarify Your Purpose

The first step in aligning your actions with your higher purpose is to clarify what that purpose is. Take time to reflect on what truly matters to you. What is the deeper reason for why you do what you do? Is it to gain wealth, status, or recognition? Or is it to contribute to the well-being of others, to live in harmony with your values, or to create something meaningful that will have a positive impact on the world?

Spend some time journaling or meditating on these questions. It's important to be honest with yourself about your motivations. Once you have a clear sense of your purpose, you can begin to make choices that reflect that purpose and guide your actions accordingly.

2. Act with Integrity

Integrity is a cornerstone of spiritual success. In every situation, strive to choose actions that align with your values. This may mean resisting the temptation to cut corners or compromise your principles for short-term gain. True success is not about achieving your goals at any cost; it is about achieving your goals while maintaining your integrity and staying true to your values.

Ask yourself: In what ways can I act with greater integrity today? Are there situations where I'm tempted to compromise my principles for the sake of convenience or financial gain? How can I stay true to my values in the face of external pressures?

3. Serve the Greater Good

Another key aspect of spiritual success is the focus on service. True success is found in the ability to serve others and contribute to the collective well-being. When you focus on helping others, whether through your work, relationships, or community involvement, you generate positive karm that will come back to you in the form of fulfillment, joy, and a sense of purpose.

Ask yourself: How does my work benefit others? In what ways can I contribute to the greater good? What can I do today to make a positive impact on the people around me?

4. Stay Present in the Process

Often, we become so focused on the end goal that we forget to enjoy the process. We chase after success, thinking that happiness lies in the future when we achieve our goals. But true success is found in the journey itself—in the way we live each moment, in the choices we make, and in the attitude we bring to our work and relationships.

Instead of fixating on the outcome, stay present in the process. Trust that the actions you take today will align you with the future success you desire. Enjoy the growth, learning, and personal development that happen along the way.

Reflection Exercise: Redefining Success

Take some time to reflect on what success truly means to you. Is your view of success based purely on material achievements, or is it tied to something deeper—like contributing to the well-being of others or fulfilling your life's purpose?

Use the following questions to guide your reflection:

1. What are the key values that drive me?
2. How can I live in alignment with those values?
3. What does success look like if it's not just about wealth, status, or fame?
4. How can I use my unique talents and skills to contribute to the greater good?

Action with Purpose

Think about one area of your life—whether career, relationships, or personal growth—and reflect on how you can align your actions with your higher purpose. Write down specific actions you can take to ensure that your decisions are in alignment with your values. Set clear intentions for how you want to show up in the world and start taking small steps toward living in alignment with your true purpose.

VIII

The Law of Attraction and Karm: Manifesting with Purpose

Introduction: The Intersection of the Law of Attraction and Karm

The Law of Attraction and Karm are two of the most powerful forces that shape our lives. Both are universal laws that govern our experiences, but when understood together, they become even more transformative. The Law of Attraction suggests that our thoughts and feelings attract similar energy from the universe, while Karm focuses on the cause-and-effect principle, where our actions, thoughts, and words create consequences, whether positive or negative.

While these laws might seem separate, they work together in a harmonious cycle to bring about the reality we experience. If we focus on good thoughts and actions, we are aligning ourselves with the Law of Attraction, which will bring positive manifestations into our lives. However, if our past actions have created negative karmic imprints, we may find our desires blocked or delayed, even with positive thinking.

This chapter will explore the dynamic interplay between Karm and the Law of Attraction, focusing on how we can leverage both forces to manifest our desires in alignment with our true purpose.

The Power of Intention and Thought

To begin understanding how these two forces work together, it's essential to look at thoughts and intentions. The Law of Attraction states that what we focus on expands. However, this focus must be rooted in clarity and positive intent.

1. **Focused Thoughts and Positive Energy:** Our thoughts hold power, and the energy we create with them attracts similar energy. For example, if you focus on feelings of gratitude and abundance, the universe will respond by sending more things into your life that you are grateful for. This is the Law of Attraction at work.
2. **Intentionality as the Key to Manifestation:** Intentions go a step beyond mere thoughts. An intention is a focused thought with purpose. It's a commitment you make to yourself to manifest a certain outcome. Whether it's a personal goal like attracting love, or a professional goal like increasing wealth, setting an

intention provides a clear roadmap for what you want to bring into your life.

However, Karm can affect your ability to manifest those intentions. If you have negative karmic imprints from past actions (unresolved anger, resentment, dishonesty, etc.), these can create resistance. This resistance will make it harder to manifest your desires, no matter how much you focus on them.

Clearing Karmic Blockages for Clearer Manifestation

The first step in merging the Law of Attraction with Karm is to clear your karmic blockages. Often, we carry emotional baggage or unresolved karm that prevents us from fully manifesting the life we want. These karmic blockages are like heavy weights on our energy field, slowing down the manifestation process.

1. **Forgiveness:** Forgiving yourself and others is one of the most powerful tools for clearing negative karm. Holding onto grudges, anger, or past pain creates an energetic block in your body and mind. The Law of Attraction cannot work fully if you are still holding onto resentment. By forgiving, you release this negative energy and allow new, positive energy to flow in.
2. **Healing Past Mistakes:** Sometimes, the karm we carry is the result of our own actions that hurt others. If you've made mistakes in the past—whether it's lying, cheating, or other harmful actions—these can create a karmic debt. To clear this debt, you can take responsibility for your actions, seek forgiveness from those affected, and

actively work on being a better version of yourself moving forward.

3. **Mindfulness and Self-Awareness:** Being mindful of the patterns and behaviours that contribute to negative karm is essential. Self-awareness allows you to make conscious choices that align with your highest good and purpose. If you catch yourself engaging in negative thinking, you can correct it and redirect your energy toward positive manifestation.

The Role of Aligned Action in Manifestation

The Law of Attraction is not about wishful thinking or passive waiting for things to magically appear in your life. It's about taking aligned action. This means that, after setting an intention, you must also take proactive steps toward your goal. These actions should be in harmony with the desires you want to manifest.

However, it's important to recognize that karmic actions also play a role here. For example, if you've been acting in self-interest or manipulative ways in the past, those actions will create karmic consequences that block the flow of manifestation. To align your actions with your desires, you must first clear any negative karmic influences from your past actions.

Here are some ways to ensure your actions are aligned with your intentions:

1. **Right Action:** Act in a way that is ethical, compassionate, and in alignment with your values. Every action, whether large or small, should move you closer to your manifestation goal.

2. **Small Steps Lead to Big Results:** Take consistent, deliberate actions towards your goal. Whether it's making a phone call, writing an email, or doing research, every small step adds up and helps bring your manifestations into reality.
3. **Let Go of Attachment to Results:** One of the most important aspects of manifesting with purpose is to release attachment to the outcome. By focusing on the process and trusting the universe, you allow the Law of Attraction to bring you the perfect results, even if they are different from what you expected.

The Power of Gratitude and Abundance

Another crucial aspect of manifestation and karm is the practice of gratitude. Gratitude is one of the highest vibrational energies you can emit. When you are grateful for what you have, the universe responds by giving you more to be grateful for.

1. **Gratitude as a Magnet:** Gratitude is magnetic. When you focus on the things you already have, whether it's your health, family, or a small achievement, you raise your energetic vibration. This creates an energy field that is attractive to more good things.
2. **Abundance vs. Scarcity Mind-set:** If you focus on the idea of lack, which is exactly what you will attract more of. Conversely, when you adopt an abundance mind-set, you begin to see endless opportunities. Abundance is not just about money—it's about love, support, and opportunity. By practicing gratitude, you align with abundance and send out a vibration that attracts more

abundance into your life.

The Role of Compassion and Service in Manifestation

True manifestation is not just about personal gain. Service to others and compassion play key roles in this process. Karm teaches us that when we serve others, we create positive karmic energy that can come back to us in the form of blessings. The Law of Attraction works more powerfully when we are working with the universe's flow of love, kindness, and compassion.

1. **Giving Freely:** The more we give without expectation, the more we receive. This can include giving time, love, or resources to others. As we serve others, we cultivate positive karm and attract more prosperity and success into our own lives.
2. **Elevating Others:** Helping others manifest their desires not only elevates them but also elevates your own energy and frequency. By helping someone achieve their goals, you create a ripple effect that positively impacts your own manifestation process.

Deepening Your Connection with the Universe

When you understand that the universe is always responding to your thoughts, feelings, and actions, it becomes easier to align yourself with its flow. The Law of Attraction and Karm work together to guide you on your journey of manifestation. However, this requires patience, faith, and trust that everything is unfolding as it should.

1. **Trusting the Process:** Often, when we desire something, we want it immediately. However, the universe may take its time to deliver, ensuring that it arrives at the right moment. Trust that everything is aligning perfectly, even if you cannot see the full picture just yet.
2. **Faith in the Universe:** Having faith that the universe will deliver is crucial. You are part of a larger plan, and sometimes things need to happen in a certain order for your manifestations to fully materialize.
3. **Surrendering to Divine Timing:** Let go of the need to control every aspect of your manifestation journey. Surrendering to divine timing means trusting that what's meant for you will come at the right moment, and that everything that happens is part of a greater process.

Conclusion

Manifesting with purpose means aligning your thoughts, actions, and intentions with both the Law of Attraction and Karm. By cultivating positive karm, clearing blockages, and taking aligned action, you create the conditions for the universe to deliver your desires. At the same time, practicing gratitude, service, and compassion ensures that your manifestations are in alignment with your highest good.

As you continue your journey, remember that manifestation is not just about receiving—it's about co-creating with the universe. The more aligned you are with your higher self and with the flow of karm, the more effortlessly the Law of Attraction will work in your favour.

IX

Karm and Health: The Mind-Body Connection

In today's world, physical health is often treated as a purely biological issue—an imbalance in the body that needs to be fixed through medicine, surgery, or lifestyle changes. While these approaches are essential for maintaining well-being, many spiritual traditions understand health as a far more complex and interconnected experience. In these traditions, the physical body is viewed not just as a vessel, but as a reflection of one's emotional, mental, and spiritual state. Health is seen as an expression of harmony or disharmony between the mind, body, and spirit.

This chapter explores the spiritual roots of physical health, particularly through the lens of karmic influences. We will look at how unresolved emotions and mental patterns can manifest as physical ailments and how understanding the connection between Karm and health can offer a deeper, holistic approach to healing. By addressing the root causes of disease—often found in past actions, unresolved emotions, and unhealed spiritual wounds—we can transform not only our physical health but also our emotional and spiritual well-being.

The Mind-Body Connection and the Role of Karm

One of the fundamental teachings of many spiritual traditions is that the mind and body are deeply interconnected. This connection is not merely metaphorical but also physiological. Our thoughts, emotions, and mental states have a direct impact on our physical health. The ancient wisdom of yoga, traditional Chinese medicine, and Ayurveda, for example, all emphasize the importance of emotional balance and mental clarity in maintaining physical health.

In the context of Karm, this interconnection is even more profound. Karm, or the law of cause and effect, suggests that the actions, thoughts, and intentions we carry throughout our lives—whether conscious or unconscious—can have a lasting impact on our bodies. These influences accumulate over time, sometimes leading to physical manifestations of unresolved emotional or mental blockages.

Negative emotions such as anger, fear, guilt, or shame are particularly potent sources of karmic imbalance. They have the ability to accumulate in the body, creating physical blockages or even diseases. For example, a person who constantly suppresses anger may experience chronic pain in the neck, shoulders, or back—areas where tension often builds up in response to emotional stress. Similarly, someone with unresolved guilt may develop digestive issues, as the body's inability to process emotions could extend to its inability to process food.

On the other hand, positive emotions such as love, compassion, peace, and gratitude are healing forces. They help to release tension, increase circulation, and promote cellular regeneration. When we align our actions and thoughts with these positive emotions, we are not only creating a more peaceful inner world, but we are also fostering a healthier physical body.

Thus, understanding Karm and its role in the mind-body connection is essential for anyone seeking a more holistic approach to health. Healing becomes more than just treating symptoms; it involves addressing the root causes of illness—our mental patterns, emotional wounds, and spiritual imbalances.

The Manifestation of Karmic Imbalances in the Body

The body serves as a mirror to the mind and soul. It reflects the inner state of being, carrying the energetic imprints of past actions, unresolved emotions, and unhealed spiritual wounds. These karmic imbalances can manifest in the body in a variety of ways, including physical illness, chronic pain, or emotional difficulties.

The Role of Emotional Blockages

One of the most powerful ways that Karm impacts health is through emotional blockages. Emotions such as fear, anger, resentment, grief, and guilt often create energetic blockages in the body. These blockages can lead to physical ailments when left unresolved over time. For instance:

Anger may manifest as tension in the liver, gallbladder, and stomach, areas traditionally associated with the body's ability to process and release negative emotions. Chronic anger can contribute to digestive issues or even liver diseases.

Fear tends to manifest in the kidneys and bladder, organs associated with the body's fight-or-flight response. Prolonged fear can lead to kidney stones, urinary tract infections, or adrenal exhaustion.

Guilt and shame can manifest in the digestive system, particularly in the stomach and intestines, which process not just food, but also emotional experiences. This could lead to conditions like ulcers, irritable bowel syndrome (IBS), or other chronic digestive disorders.

When we carry these negative emotions without processing or releasing them, they become stored in the body, creating physical imbalances that can be difficult to address through conventional medicine alone.

The Role of Unhealed Karmic Patterns

Karmic patterns also influence our health in ways that may not be immediately obvious. These patterns may stem from past experiences, either from this lifetime or previous ones. For example, a person who has experienced trauma or abandonment might have a deep-seated fear of rejection, which could manifest as physical symptoms related to the heart or lungs, the organs associated with love and connection.

In other cases, karmic imbalances might manifest as recurring health issues that seem to have no logical explanation. These could be signs that unresolved karmic lessons are being repeated in the body, and that there is a need for healing on a deeper level. Addressing these karmic patterns involves more than just treating the physical symptoms; it requires a holistic approach that includes emotional healing, forgiveness, and spiritual growth.

Karmic Lessons through Illness: Understanding the Messages

Illness and injury are often seen as messages from the body—signals that something is out of balance. While conventional medicine tends to focus on diagnosing and treating the symptoms of illness, spiritual traditions encourage us to look deeper and explore the emotional and spiritual lessons behind the disease.

By examining the emotional and mental patterns that may have contributed to the illness, we can uncover hidden karmic lessons. Each health issue can be seen as an opportunity for growth, transformation, and healing. For example:

Chronic Illness as a Call for Change

Chronic illnesses like autoimmune diseases, diabetes, or fibromyalgia can often be linked to long-standing emotional or mental stress. These illnesses may be the body's way of signaling that the person is out of alignment with their true purpose or is neglecting their emotional or spiritual needs. For instance, someone who is constantly overworking and neglecting their own needs may develop an autoimmune disorder, which involves the body attacking its own cells. This could be seen as a reflection of self-attack or self-neglect, rooted in unresolved emotional or spiritual issues.

Emotional Trauma and Heart Health

Heart disease is another area where karmic patterns can become manifest. A person who has experienced emotional trauma or who has lived with deep resentment, guilt, or grief may develop high blood pressure, heart disease, or other cardiovascular issues. The heart, often seen as the seat of love and emotional balance, reflects how we handle our emotional energy. If someone has been holding onto unprocessed emotional pain for years, this may create physical imbalances in the heart and circulatory system.

The Connection Between the Mind and Chronic Pain

Chronic pain, such as back pain, migraines, or joint pain, is often linked to emotional issues such as unresolved grief, anger, or fear. For example, lower back pain may be linked to financial stress or fear about one's security, while neck and shoulder pain may indicate unresolved anger or emotional tension. These physical manifestations are often tied to emotional energy that is being stored in the body. Addressing the emotional cause of the pain can help to relieve the physical symptoms.

Practical Steps for Healing Through Karm

Now that we understand the connection between Karm, emotional blockages, and physical health, it's important to explore practical steps we can take to heal on all levels—physical, emotional, and spiritual. These steps go beyond simply treating the symptoms and focus on addressing the root causes of illness and imbalance.

1. Listen to Your Body

The first step in healing through Karm is to develop a deeper awareness of the body. The body is constantly sending us messages about its needs and imbalances. Pay attention to any areas of discomfort, pain, or tension, and ask yourself what emotional or spiritual lesson might be behind it. For example, if you have chronic neck pain, reflect on whether you are holding onto anger or frustration. If you experience digestive issues, consider whether unresolved guilt or fear might be influencing your health.

2. Emotional Release Practices

Once you have identified the emotional blockages or mental patterns contributing to your physical health, the next step is to release them. Practices such as journaling, meditation, and breathwork can help to clear emotional blockages and release pent-up energy. These practices allow you to process and let go of negative emotions, clearing the path for healing to take place.

Journaling: Write about your feelings and experiences without judgment. Allow yourself to express any unresolved emotions, such as anger, fear, or sadness. Writing can help to release the energy associated with these emotions and create space for healing.

Meditation: Spend time each day meditating to connect with your body and emotions. As you meditate, focus on the areas of the body that feel tense or painful, and visualize light or energy flowing into those areas to release blockages.

Breathwork: Use conscious breathing techniques to release emotional tension and increase oxygen flow to the body. Deep breathing can help to calm the nervous system and promote relaxation.

3. Forgiveness for Healing

Forgiveness is one of the most powerful tools for healing the body. Holding onto resentment, guilt, or anger can have serious physical consequences, as these emotions can create blockages in the body's energy system. By forgiving others and yourself, you free up space for healing energy to flow through your body.

Practice forgiveness by reflecting on past experiences that may be causing you emotional pain. Visualize yourself releasing the emotional charge associated with these memories. Forgiveness does not mean condoning harmful actions, but rather releasing the grip that those emotions have on your body and mind.

4. Holistic Approaches to Health

Incorporating holistic practices into your life can help clear karmic blockages and restore balance to your body, mind, and spirit. These practices nurture the body from all angles and encourage deep healing:

Yoga: Yoga helps to release tension, improve flexibility, and balance energy in the body. Many yoga practices focus on breathing and mindfulness, which can aid in emotional release and mental clarity.

Acupuncture: This ancient healing art can help clear energetic blockages and restore balance to the body's energy flow. It is especially useful for addressing emotional or spiritual imbalances that may be contributing to physical symptoms.

Reiki and Energy Healing: These practices work by channeling healing energy into the body to clear blockages and promote balance. Reiki can help heal emotional wounds and release stagnant energy that may be causing physical pain.

Reflection Exercise

To deepen your understanding of how emotional and spiritual blockages may be influencing your health, engage in the following exercises:

Body Awareness: Sit quietly and take a few deep breaths. Slowly scan your body from head to toe, paying attention to any areas of discomfort, tension, or pain. Gently ask yourself what emotional experiences or thoughts might be contributing to this physical sensation. Write down any insights that arise.

Healing Through Forgiveness: Identify any people or situations in your life that you are holding onto negative emotions toward. Practice forgiveness in your heart, visualizing yourself releasing the emotional charge attached to these past experiences. Allow yourself to feel the freedom and lightness that comes with letting go.

Conclusion

As we have explored throughout this chapter, the connection between Karm, emotional health, and physical health is profound and powerful. Illnesses and ailments are not just random occurrences—they are often karmic lessons or manifestations of unresolved emotional blockages. By understanding the deeper spiritual and emotional causes of our physical health, we can heal not just the body, but the mind and spirit as well. Through practices such as emotional release, forgiveness, and holistic healing, we can clear karmic imbalances and restore balance to our bodies, leading to greater health, peace, and well-being.

X

Meditation and Mindfulness: Unlocking the Power of the Present Moment

Meditation is one of the most powerful tools available for understanding and transforming our karmic patterns. In spiritual traditions, meditation is seen not just as a method of relaxation or stress relief, but as a transformative practice that allows us to directly engage with the deeper layers of our consciousness. By cultivating a still mind, we create space for introspection and insight, which in turn helps us unravel the karmic imprints left by our past actions, thoughts, and emotions.

Karm, the law of cause and effect, governs much of our experience, including our health, relationships, and even our inner peace. While many of us are aware of the obvious consequences of our actions, meditation offers a way to examine the subtle karmic influences that shape our lives in unconscious and often hidden ways. Through regular meditation, we begin to develop the self-awareness needed to recognize and release these negative patterns, leading to profound personal transformation.

Meditation and the Nature of Karm

Karm can be understood as a collection of energetic imprints left by our actions, thoughts, and intentions. These imprints, while often invisible, influence our experiences and interactions in the world. In the same way that the law of gravity dictates the motion of objects in the physical world, the law of Karm dictates the flow of energy in our lives. Every thought, every emotion, every decision creates a ripple that can have lasting effects.

However, Karm is not just about external consequences—it is also about the internal landscape of our mind and spirit. Our Karm shapes the way we perceive the world, the way we respond to situations, and even the way we experience emotions. While we cannot change the past, we do have the power to transform the present moment, and this is where meditation plays a key role.

By cultivating mindfulness and awareness through meditation, we gain access to deeper layers of the self that may have been hidden by layers of emotional reactivity, unconscious patterns, or past traumas. As we meditate, we begin to observe the thoughts and emotions that rise within us—thoughts that are often driven by past experiences and karmic patterns. Once we become aware of these patterns, we can choose to release them and consciously redirect our energy toward more positive and intentional actions.

The Power of Meditation in Clearing Karmic Blockages

Meditation offers a direct path to self-awareness, and through this heightened awareness, we can identify the sources of karmic imbalances. These imbalances often arise from unresolved emotions, unhealed wounds, and mental habits that no longer serve us. Once we recognize these patterns, we can begin the process of healing by releasing the energy they hold and making conscious choices to create new, more harmonious karmic imprints.

Karmic blockages can take many forms. They might appear as physical ailments, emotional struggles, or relational difficulties. In some cases, they may manifest as recurring negative patterns in our thoughts or behaviors, such as chronic fear, anger, or self-doubt. These patterns, while not always easy to detect, are often driven by past unresolved Karm. Through meditation, we can begin to bring awareness to these blockages and heal them at their source.

One of the most transformative aspects of meditation is its ability to help us detach from our old, limiting beliefs and emotions. When we meditate, we create space between our thoughts and our identities, allowing us to see our habitual reactions as just that—habits, not truths. This awareness allows us to consciously break free from the karmic patterns that have held us captive, opening the door to new possibilities and experiences.

The Practice of Mindfulness

Mindfulness is the practice of being fully present and aware in the moment. While this concept has gained significant popularity in recent years, it is an ancient practice that forms the foundation of many meditation traditions. Mindfulness involves observing our thoughts, emotions, and behaviors without judgment or attachment. Through mindfulness, we can develop the ability to step back from our habitual reactions and become more conscious of the choices we make in every moment.

Mindfulness is especially important when it comes to karmic transformation. Our karmic patterns are often unconscious and automatic. For example, when we experience a stressful situation, we may automatically react with anger, fear, or defensiveness. These reactions are often rooted in past experiences or traumas, and they are fueled by the karmic imprints of those experiences.

When we practice mindfulness, we can begin to notice these automatic reactions as they arise. Instead of simply reacting, we create space to pause, reflect, and choose a different response—one that is in alignment with our highest intentions. This moment of pause allows us to interrupt the cycle of negative Karm and replace it with more conscious, positive actions.

Mindfulness helps us stay grounded in the present moment, where true transformation occurs. The present is the only time we have the power to make new choices and create new karmic imprints. When we are caught in the past—through regret, guilt, or unresolved trauma—or when we are anxious about the future, we lose our connection to the present moment. The present moment is where healing happens, where we can release old patterns and create new ones.

By practicing mindfulness regularly, we develop the ability to see beyond our habitual reactions and beliefs. We become more attuned to the subtle shifts in our thoughts and emotions, and we begin to understand the deeper causes of our karmic patterns. This awareness allows us to heal old wounds and transform our lives on a much deeper level.

A Simple Meditation for Clearing Karmic Blockages

For those who are seeking to clear their karmic imprints and release negative energy, meditation can be an incredibly powerful tool. One simple yet effective practice is a meditation specifically designed to heal past wounds and reset your energetic state. Below is a step-by-step guide to a meditation for clearing karmic blockages.

1. **Find a Quiet Space**

To begin, find a quiet space where you can sit comfortably without distractions. Make sure that your posture is upright and that you feel relaxed yet alert. Close your eyes and take several deep breaths, allowing each exhale to release any tension in your body. Feel your body relax with each breath, becoming more grounded and centered.

2. **Focus on Your Heart**

Bring your awareness to your heart space. Imagine a warm, loving light radiating from your heart, expanding with each breath you take. This light represents unconditional love, the most potent force for clearing negative Karm. Allow this light to fill your entire being, healing and purifying every cell, every thought, and every emotion.

3. **Reflect on Your Actions**

As you continue to breathe deeply, reflect on any negative karmic patterns you may have been holding onto. This might include feelings of resentment, guilt, fear, or anger. Acknowledge these feelings without judgment, knowing that they are part of your journey, but that they no longer serve you. Accept them as they are, and give yourself permission to release them.

4. **Release the Negative Energy**

With each exhale, imagine that you are releasing all of the negative energy tied to your past actions and thoughts. Visualize this karmic energy dissolving into the light of your heart, where it is transmuted into love, compassion, and forgiveness. As you continue to breathe, feel the heaviness lift from your body and your mind, replaced by lightness and peace.

5. **Set an Intention for Positive Karm**

Once you have released the old, set an intention for how you wish to live moving forward. This could be an intention of love, abundance, peace, joy, or any quality that resonates with your highest self. Imagine this intention expanding from your heart, filling your entire being with positive energy. Visualize it radiating outward, creating a ripple of positive Karm that extends to everyone you encounter.

6. **End with Gratitude**

Take a few moments to express gratitude for the opportunity to clear your karmic imprints and create new, positive actions. Feel a deep sense of peace and openness to the new energy you are inviting into your life. With each breath, acknowledge the power of this moment and the transformation that has already begun.

This meditation can be practiced regularly to help release karmic blockages and reset your energetic state. Over time, as you continue to meditate and practice mindfulness, you will notice a shift in your experience. Old patterns of fear, anger, and resentment will lose their grip on you, and you will begin to attract more positive energy into your life.

Benefits of Regular Meditation for Karmic Healing

Regular meditation practice has a wide range of benefits, particularly when it comes to understanding and transforming Karm. Some of the key benefits include:

Increased Self-Awareness

Meditation helps us develop a deeper awareness of our thoughts, emotions, and behaviors. By cultivating mindfulness, we can recognize unconscious habits that perpetuate negative karmic patterns. Through this self-awareness, we gain the ability to make more conscious choices and release harmful patterns that no longer serve us.

Emotional Healing

Meditation offers a powerful tool for emotional healing. By meditating regularly, we can clear emotional baggage and heal old wounds that contribute to negative karmic patterns. This emotional healing is essential for breaking free from past traumas and moving forward with a clean slate.

Clarity and Insight

Meditation provides clarity about our purpose, direction, and the actions we need to take to align with our highest intentions. It helps us gain insight into our karmic patterns and understand the deeper causes of our experiences. This clarity allows us to make more intentional choices and align our actions with our true purpose.

Manifestation Power

When the mind is calm and centered, it becomes easier to focus on the positive and to manifest our desires effectively. Meditation helps us clear the mental clutter and align our energy with our highest intentions, making it easier to manifest the life we want to create. By focusing on love, peace, and abundance, we can attract more of these qualities into our lives.

Conclusion

Meditation is a powerful tool for understanding and transforming our Karm. By cultivating mindfulness and self-awareness, we can identify the karmic patterns that shape our lives and begin to release them. Through regular meditation practice, we can heal emotional wounds, gain clarity and insight, and manifest a more positive and intentional life. Whether you are new to meditation or have been practicing for years, the power of meditation to transform your karmic imprints is undeniable. Through meditation, we can create a new reality—one that is filled with love, peace, and abundance.

XI

Surrender: The Art of Letting Go and Trusting the Flow

Surrender is a concept that has been discussed in various spiritual, psychological, and philosophical traditions. However, it is often misunderstood in modern culture, particularly in the context of personal growth and achieving success. For many, surrender is equated with weakness, passivity, or resignation—an act of giving up, an admission of defeat. Yet, in the deeper spiritual sense, surrender is not about giving up, but about letting go of the ego's need to control the flow of life and instead aligning oneself with a higher purpose. When viewed through the lens of karm, surrender becomes a conscious choice to trust the process of life, understanding that not everything is within our control and that many events are unfolding according to karmic laws beyond our individual actions.

In this chapter, we explore the meaning of surrender within the context of karm, and how it can facilitate spiritual growth, healing, and a deeper understanding of life's natural flow. We will look at how surrender and manifestation are paradoxically intertwined, and how letting go of attachment to outcomes can help us live more freely and harmoniously with the universe.

The True Nature of Surrender

Surrender, as defined in many spiritual traditions, is the act of letting go of attachment and control, particularly in relation to external events and outcomes. It is not about becoming passive or disengaged from life but about allowing ourselves to accept life's natural flow without interference from the ego. In its truest sense, surrender is an acknowledgment that we are part of a larger whole—an infinite web of existence—where every moment is connected to the past, the present, and the future.

In the context of karm, surrender means releasing the need to control every outcome of our actions, thoughts, or emotions. karm, which refers to the law of cause and effect, tells us that everything we do, say, or think creates an energy imprint that will eventually return to us. But often, this return is beyond our understanding or control, as it unfolds according to the natural law of cosmic order. Surrendering to this flow allows us to stop fighting against the consequences of our past actions and instead trust that the unfolding of our karmic path is aligned with the greater good for ourselves and others.

The Bhagavad Gita, one of the central texts in Hindu philosophy, beautifully encapsulates the essence of surrender. Lord Krishna advises Arjuna to perform his duties without attachment to the results. He teaches that true liberation comes from the act of surrendering to the Divine Will, where one acts from a place of devotion and detachment, trusting that the Universe will guide the course of their life. This principle is not about inaction, but about shifting from a mindset of control to one of trust.

Karm and the Role of Surrender

Understanding surrender in relation to karm requires a deeper exploration of how karm operates in our lives. karm is not simply a punitive force; it is the flow of energy that results from our actions, thoughts, and emotions. These energetic imprints, whether positive or negative, continue to influence our present and future experiences. While we are not always in control of the karmic seeds we have planted in the past, we can choose how we respond to their consequences.

Our responses to life's challenges and rewards are deeply connected to our karmic patterns. If we constantly react with fear, anger, or resentment, we are reinforcing negative karm, which will, in turn, lead to more situations that provoke similar responses. On the other hand, if we respond with patience, grace, acceptance, and trust, we create positive karm that can help us navigate the flow of life with ease and harmony.

Surrender allows us to release the karmic grip of resistance. Resistance is often rooted in the ego's desire to control or manipulate outcomes. We may resist the consequences of our past actions or the unfolding of life's challenges because we fear that they will bring suffering, discomfort, or pain. However, when we resist life's flow, we compound our karm, perpetuating cycles of struggle and frustration. Surrender, on the other hand, invites us to accept what is, knowing that even our current situation holds valuable lessons and that the universe has a way of guiding us toward growth and healing.

When we surrender, we stop resisting the flow of life. We let go of the need to force things to happen on our timeline or according to our preferences. Instead, we open ourselves to the wisdom and opportunities that arise naturally from each moment. Surrendering doesn't mean that we are passive bystanders in our lives; rather, it means we are active participants, consciously choosing to trust the unfolding of life and release attachment to outcomes.

The Paradox of Control and Surrender

At the heart of surrender lies the paradox of control and letting go. On one hand, we are taught that in order to manifest our desires, we must set clear intentions, take action, and work toward our goals. On the other hand, we are also told to surrender our attachment to outcomes and trust the timing and flow of the universe. This paradox can be confusing: How do we balance taking inspired action with letting go of attachment? Is it possible to act while surrendering at the same time?

The key lies in understanding that true surrender is not about inaction, but about aligning our actions with the natural flow of life. It is about making conscious choices that are in harmony with our values and desires, while simultaneously relinquishing control over how and when things will unfold.

One of the most powerful aspects of manifestation is the ability to set clear intentions. When we focus on what we want to create, we align our energy and actions with that goal. However, if we become overly attached to how or when our desires will manifest, we create resistance. Resistance blocks the flow of energy and prevents the universe from aligning the perfect circumstances for us. This is where surrender becomes essential.

Take, for example, Simran, a young entrepreneur who worked tirelessly to launch her online business. She had set clear intentions, worked long hours, and visualized her success. Yet, after several months of little progress, she became frustrated and anxious. The more she pushed, the more resistance she encountered. Simran's attachment to the outcome of her business was causing her stress and limiting her ability to see new opportunities.

It wasn't until she decided to surrender that things began to shift. Simran took a step back, focusing on enjoying the process of building her business rather than obsessing over the outcome. She stopped forcing things to happen and began trusting that the universe would guide her to the right opportunities at the right time. Within a few weeks, opportunities began to appear, perfectly aligned with her goals—only after she stopped trying to control every aspect of her journey. This is the power of surrender: letting go of the need to control the "how" and "when," and allowing the universe to unfold its blessings in its own perfect timing.

Practical Ways to Practice Surrender

While the concept of surrender can be abstract, there are practical ways to begin integrating it into your daily life. The following steps can help you practice surrender in a way that is both grounding and empowering.

1. Let Go of the Need for Control

Recognize that you cannot control every aspect of your life. There will always be factors outside your control—whether it's the actions of others, the timing of events, or the outcome of your efforts. Surrendering means trusting that the universe is guiding you and that everything is unfolding as it should. Focus on what you can control—your thoughts, actions, and reactions—and let go of the need to manipulate the circumstances beyond your control.

2. Release Attachment to Outcomes

While it's important to set clear intentions and take inspired action, it's equally important to release attachment to specific outcomes. Trust that the universe will provide you with what is needed for your highest good, even if it's not in the form or timeline that you expect. Practice detachment by embracing uncertainty and remaining open to unexpected blessings.

3. Embrace the Flow of Life

Life is full of ups and downs, successes and failures, joys and challenges. Embrace this flow and trust that each moment serves a purpose in your journey. Whether you're experiencing the crest of a wave or the trough, know that each experience is guiding you toward growth. Surrendering means embracing both the highs and lows with grace and acceptance.

4. Practice Gratitude for Uncertainty

Uncertainty can feel uncomfortable, but it is also where transformation and growth happen. Instead of resisting the unknown, practice gratitude for it. Trust that the mystery of life holds wisdom and that you are being guided in the right direction. Gratitude helps shift your perspective, allowing you to embrace life's uncertainties with an open heart.

A Meditation for Surrender

To deepen your experience of surrender, try the following meditation. This practice will help you release attachments and trust the flow of life.

1. Find Your Centre

Sit comfortably in a quiet space. Close your eyes and take several deep breaths. Focus on your breath as it moves in and out, grounding yourself in the present moment.

2. Visualize the Flow

Imagine a peaceful river flowing through a lush forest. See your desires, goals, and fears floating on the surface of the water. As you breathe, see these thoughts and desires drifting away, carried by the current. Trust that they are moving toward their rightful place in the universe.

3. Release Attachment

Feel yourself letting go of the need to control how things will unfold. Visualize yourself surrendering to the flow, releasing all attachment to specific outcomes. Trust that the universe will provide what you need at the perfect time.

4. Affirm Trust

Repeat silently: "I trust in the flow of life. I release all resistance and embrace the unknown with an open heart." Feel your body relax deeper into the surrender, knowing that you are supported in all ways.

5. End with Gratitude

As you conclude the meditation, express gratitude for the opportunity to practice surrender. Thank the universe for its guidance and trust that whatever is meant for you will come in perfect timing and form.

Conclusion

Surrender is a powerful tool for navigating the complexities of karm and life's challenges. By releasing attachment and trusting in the universe's flow, we align ourselves with a higher purpose and invite more peace and fulfillment into our lives. Surrender is not about passivity or resignation; it is about embracing the natural flow of life with trust and acceptance. Through regular practice of surrender, we can release resistance, heal karmic wounds, and step into a life of greater ease, joy, and alignment with our highest self.

XII

The Importance of Self-Love in Transforming Karm

Introduction

Healing the self through love is one of the most profound journeys we can embark on in our lifetime. The transformative power of self-love cannot be overstated. It serves as the cornerstone of emotional, mental, and spiritual healing, directly influencing the way we interact with the world around us. If we do not practice self-love, we may unknowingly continue to repeat harmful patterns, attract negative situations, and stay locked in cycles of unresolved pain. On the other hand, when we nurture self-love, we open ourselves to profound healing, personal growth, and positive transformation.

At its core, self-love is about recognizing your inherent worth, treating yourself with kindness and compassion, and embracing your unique qualities—flaws and all. This chapter delves deeply into the process of cultivating self-love and how it lays the foundation for healing. We will explore practical steps to nurture self-love, as well as the spiritual and psychological benefits of embracing this practice fully.

The Connection Between Self-Love and Healing

The link between self-love and healing is both spiritual and psychological. The concept of karm, which refers to the law of cause and effect, plays a significant role in our healing journey. When we choose to love ourselves, we break free from the karmic cycles that perpetuate suffering. Self-love creates a protective shield around us, allowing us to act in alignment with our highest values and desires, instead of being governed by past patterns, self-doubt, and fear.

When we practice self-love, we shift the energy we project into the world. The energy of love is transformative—it is a high-frequency vibration that attracts positivity, peace, and abundance. This shift in energy not only impacts how we perceive ourselves but also influences how others perceive and interact with us. By embracing self-love, we stop seeking validation externally and begin to create a life based on our own internal compass.

Moreover, self-love fosters self-acceptance. This means acknowledging our strengths and weaknesses without judgment. It is about being kind to ourselves, especially during times of struggle or failure. When we accept ourselves completely, we give ourselves permission to heal, grow, and evolve without the burden of unrealistic expectations or self-criticism.

The Psychological Basis of Self-Love

Psychologically, self-love is linked to healthy self-esteem, self-worth, and emotional resilience. People with high self-love are less likely to fall into patterns of self-destructive behavior or attract toxic relationships because they have a strong sense of their own value. Self-love nurtures the belief that we are worthy of happiness, success, and all good things in life. It is the foundation of emotional intelligence, helping us navigate difficult emotions with greater ease and balance.

When we lack self-love, we often seek approval and validation from others, which leaves us vulnerable to manipulation, emotional dependency, and feelings of inadequacy. On the other hand, self-love promotes a sense of inner security, which strengthens our ability to make decisions that align with our authentic selves, rather than trying to meet external expectations.

A lack of self-love can manifest as self-sabotage, where individuals consciously or unconsciously undermine their own happiness and success. For example, someone who doesn't love themselves may stay in an unhealthy relationship, overwork themselves to the point of burnout, or engage in harmful habits like substance abuse or negative self-talk. When we choose to practice self-love, we break these destructive cycles, allowing for emotional healing and positive growth.

The Spiritual Significance of Self-Love

Spiritually, self-love is deeply connected to the concept of divine love. Many spiritual traditions emphasize the importance of loving oneself as a pathway to connecting with the divine. By loving ourselves, we honor the divine spark within us and align ourselves with the universal energy of love that flows through all beings. This alignment with divine love brings peace, serenity, and a deep sense of fulfillment, as we begin to see ourselves as worthy of receiving love and blessings.

In many spiritual teachings, the idea of karm is integral to understanding the consequences of our actions and decisions. The law of karm suggests that everything we do, think, and say generates an energetic ripple that influences our present and future circumstances. When we practice self-love, we create positive karmic energy that attracts harmony, healing, and abundance into our lives. By choosing self-love over self-judgment, we create the space for healing past wounds and releasing old karmic debts.

Furthermore, self-love is the pathway to self-empowerment. When we recognize and honor our worth, we free ourselves from the need to seek approval or validation from external sources. We begin to act in accordance with our highest values, which leads to greater alignment with our soul's purpose. This sense of empowerment enables us to step into our full potential, heal from past traumas, and create the life we truly desire.

Practical Practices for Cultivating Self-Love

While the concept of self-love may seem abstract, there are several practical ways to nurture it in daily life. Below are four powerful practices that can help cultivate self-love and healing:

1. Affirmations: Reinforcing Your Worth

Affirmations are one of the simplest yet most effective tools for cultivating self-love. By repeating positive affirmations daily, you begin to reprogram your subconscious mind and replace negative thought patterns with loving and empowering beliefs. Affirmations serve as reminders of your inherent worth and the truth of who you are.

To start, create affirmations that resonate with you personally. Here are some examples to get you started:

"I am worthy of love, respect, and happiness."

"I honor and respect myself in all that I do."

"I am deserving of all good things in life."

"I choose to love and accept myself unconditionally."

"I trust in my ability to heal and grow."

Affirmations work best when they are repeated consistently and with intention. You can say them aloud, write them down, or meditate on them. Over time, the positive energy of the affirmations will begin to shift your mindset, helping you to embody self-love on a deeper level.

2. Self-Care: Nourishing Your Mind, Body, and Soul

Self-love is not just about thoughts; it's also about actions. One of the most important ways to demonstrate self-love is through self-care. Self-care involves taking time to nourish your mind, body, and soul, ensuring that you feel balanced, rested, and rejuvenated.

Some self-care practices include:

Physical self-care: Regular exercise, eating nutritious foods, getting enough sleep, and pampering yourself with activities like a relaxing bath or massage.

Mental self-care: Engaging in activities that stimulate your mind, such as reading, learning new skills, or engaging in creative expression like writing or painting.

Emotional self-care: Journaling, meditating, or practicing mindfulness to help you process and release any emotional blocks or negativity.

Spiritual self-care: Taking time for spiritual practices that resonate with you, such as prayer, meditation, or connecting with nature.

Self-care is not a luxury: it is a necessity. By taking care of yourself, you show your subconscious mind that you are worthy of attention, care, and love. Prioritizing self-care also helps reduce stress, increase energy levels, and improve overall well-being.

3. Forgiveness: Letting Go of Self-Judgment and Regret

A significant part of healing through self-love is practicing forgiveness—specifically, forgiving yourself. Many of us carry around deep-seated regret, guilt, and shame from past mistakes. These feelings can weigh heavily on our hearts and minds, preventing us from moving forward. The practice of self-forgiveness is crucial for healing and self-acceptance.

Forgiving yourself means recognizing that you are human, and making mistakes is a natural part of life. It is important to release the negative emotions tied to these mistakes and give yourself the grace to grow from them. Self-forgiveness does not mean excusing harmful behavior; rather, it is about acknowledging your imperfections, learning from them, and choosing to move forward with a renewed sense of self-love.

A simple practice for self-forgiveness is to write a letter to yourself. In the letter, express compassion and understanding for the mistakes you've made, and forgive yourself for them. This process can be incredibly healing, as it allows you to release any emotional burden and embrace the present moment with an open heart.

4. Boundaries: Protecting Your Energy and Prioritizing Your Needs

Healthy boundaries are a vital aspect of self-love. When we do not set clear boundaries, we may find ourselves overextended, drained, and overwhelmed. Setting boundaries allows us to protect our energy, prioritize our needs, and maintain our sense of self-worth.

Boundaries can be physical, emotional, or psychological. They involve saying "no" when necessary and creating space for yourself without feeling guilty. Boundaries also mean distancing yourself from toxic relationships or situations that drain your energy and prevent you from growing.

Some examples of setting boundaries include:

1. Saying no to requests or invitations that don't align with your values or priorities.
2. Taking time for yourself each day to recharge, even if it's just for a few minutes of quiet reflection.
3. Communicating openly and honestly with others about your limits and needs.
4. Letting go of relationships or environments that are emotionally harmful or draining.
5. By setting boundaries, you create an environment where self-love can flourish. You begin to honor your time, energy, and emotions, which leads to greater peace and emotional well-being.

Conclusion

Healing the self through love is not a destination; it is a continuous journey. By choosing to love yourself unconditionally, you pave the way for deep emotional healing, spiritual growth, and the creation of a life filled with abundance, peace, and fulfillment. The practices outlined in this chapter—affirmations, self-care, forgiveness, and boundaries—are tools that can help you build a strong foundation of self-love, allowing you to break free from karmic cycles and embrace your true potential.

Remember, self-love is not about perfection; it is about acceptance. By loving yourself fully, you open the door to healing, transformation, and the life you truly deserve.

XIII

Embracing Your Destiny: The Final Step towards Spiritual Mastery

As we approach the end of this transformative journey through karm, manifestation, meditation, and surrender, we arrive at the most profound realization: You are the creator of your destiny. Every thought, every action, every choice you've made up until now has shaped your present reality. And now, through the insights and practices shared throughout this book, you have awakened to the powerful truth that you have the ability to consciously create your future. This is where the real magic happens.

This chapter is not the conclusion of your journey; it is the beginning of your true empowerment. You are about to step fully into your role as a conscious co-creator of your life. The tools and wisdom you have gained will help you navigate the ever-unfolding path toward your highest potential. Now that you know the principles of karm and manifestation, you have the ability to transform your life from the inside out. As you integrate these teachings, subtle but profound shifts will take place, and you will begin to witness the magic of creation as it unfolds before you.

The Power of Awareness: The First Step Toward Transformation

The foundation of creating your destiny lies in awareness. Awareness is the light that illuminates the darkness of unconscious patterns. Before you can begin to transform your reality, you must first become aware of the forces shaping it. These forces may be your past karmic imprints, the beliefs that no longer serve you, or the unconscious programs running in your mind. As you bring awareness to these aspects of your life, you allow yourself the space to make conscious decisions about what you wish to keep, release, or transform.

To truly create your destiny, you must be willing to look at your life with an honest lens. This means facing the parts of yourself that are resistant to change, the parts that may be attached to old ways of being, or the parts that feel unworthy of success and happiness. These are the areas where karmic patterns often reside, influencing your actions and choices in ways that may no longer align with your highest purpose.

The more you practice awareness through meditation, reflection, and conscious intention, the more you will begin to understand the root of your present reality. This clarity is essential because, as you move forward, you will be making decisions based not on fear or old conditioning, but from a place of deep inner knowing.

The Shifts That Begin to Unfold

Once you embark on the path of conscious creation, the changes may be subtle at first, but they will be powerful. You may notice that the fear-based thoughts and ego-driven patterns that once governed your life will begin to dissolve. These patterns are often the result of unconscious karmic imprints—past experiences, limiting beliefs, and unresolved emotions—that have been carried forward into your current life.

As you let go of these old patterns, you will make space for your soul's true desires to emerge. No longer bound by the limitations of the ego, you will begin to feel a greater sense of inner peace and alignment with your higher self. Your energy will shift, and the vibration of love, abundance, and joy will begin to flow freely through you. You will attract the people, experiences, and opportunities that align with your soul's highest purpose.

This is where the true power of manifestation comes into play. When you align with your soul's true desires, manifestation becomes effortless. Your thoughts, emotions, and actions will naturally synchronize with the energy of abundance, creating a powerful flow of positive experiences. The more you trust this process, the more you will see the miraculous unfold in your life.

Surrender: Letting Go of Control

One of the most challenging aspects of conscious creation is learning to surrender. In a world that often values control and certainty, surrendering to the flow of life can feel unsettling. But true creation comes from a place of surrender. It is about releasing the need to control every aspect of your life and trusting in the divine intelligence that guides you.

Surrender is not passive; it is active trust. It is about recognizing that you are not separate from the universe, but an integral part of it. When you surrender to the flow of life, you align with the highest possible frequency, allowing the universe to bring forth the people, circumstances, and resources that will support your growth.

The process of surrender also involves letting go of attachment to outcomes. When we are attached to a specific outcome, we limit the flow of energy and block the magic that can unfold. By practicing surrender, you create space for unexpected blessings and miracles to manifest. The key is to remain open and receptive, knowing that what is meant for you will come to you in divine timing.

The Call to Action: Step Into Your Power

This moment is your invitation to step fully into your power as the co-creator of your life. You have now received the tools and wisdom to transform your karm, align with your soul's purpose, and manifest the future you've always dreamed of. The journey ahead will not always be easy, but it will be worth it. There will be moments of challenge, moments of discomfort, and moments when the old patterns of the ego try to resurface.

But remember: every challenge is an opportunity for growth, for healing, and for mastering your own energy. Each obstacle you face is simply an invitation to rise to a higher level of consciousness and self-mastery. It is in these moments that you will discover the depth of your strength and resilience.

As you move forward on this journey, trust that you are supported by a greater force—whether you call it the universe, divine intelligence, or your higher self. This force is always guiding you toward your highest good, and you are never alone. The universe is always conspiring in your favor, even when things don't seem to go according to plan.

Trust that each step you take brings you closer to the life you were meant to live. Embrace each step with faith, knowing that you are walking the path of light, guided by the love and wisdom of your soul.

The Road Ahead: What's Next?

The teachings in this book have provided the foundation for your transformation, but this is just the beginning of your journey. There is much more to discover, much more to experience, and much more to learn. The process of spiritual growth and self-discovery is ongoing, and the next phase of your evolution will take you deeper into the mysteries of the universe.

In the next edition of this work, we will explore the following advanced topics to help you further accelerate your spiritual evolution:

Advanced Meditation Practices: We will go beyond the basics of mindfulness and dive into techniques that will allow you to unlock deeper states of consciousness. These practices will enable you to access higher dimensions of awareness, receive guidance from your higher self, and cultivate profound inner peace.

The Science of Manifestation: Manifestation is not just a mystical process; it is grounded in the laws of physics and quantum mechanics. We will explore how to work with the energetic field to manifest at will, tapping into the hidden forces that govern reality.

Karmic Relationships: Relationships are often the most complex aspect of our lives, and they hold powerful lessons for our spiritual growth. We will delve into the dynamics of karmic relationships and how to navigate them from a place of conscious awareness and spiritual maturity.

Living in Alignment with Your Soul's Purpose: As you continue on your journey, you will learn how to fine-tune your life's path, stepping into the highest version of yourself. We will explore how to live with grace, ease, and purpose, manifesting your soul's true desires and living your destiny with joy and fulfillment.

Climax: The Divine Union of Karm and Destiny

The true climax of your journey is the divine union of karm and destiny. When you understand that you are both the creator and the experiencer of your own reality, the magic of life begins to unfold. This is when you stop feeling like a victim of your circumstances and begin to see yourself as the master of your fate.

No longer bound by the limiting beliefs and karmic patterns of the past, you are free to manifest your highest potential. The energy of love, peace, and abundance will flow through you effortlessly, guiding you toward your deepest desires and dreams. You will experience life as a continuous dance of creation, where every thought, every word, and every action is an expression of your divine essence.

But this journey is not just about manifesting material success or personal achievements. It is about returning to your true nature—the eternal, limitless being who is always in perfect harmony with the universe. It is about remembering that you are not separate from the universe, but an integral part of it. And when you live from this understanding, life becomes an ongoing process of creation, joy, and fulfillment.

This is the true magic of the journey: the realization that you are the creator of your destiny, and through your awareness, intention, and surrender, you have the power to create a life of infinite possibilities. Trust in yourself, trust in the process, and step boldly into the life you were always meant to live.

Conclusion

As you close this chapter, know that the journey is far from over. You have only just begun to tap into the incredible potential within you. The path ahead will be filled with endless opportunities for growth, discovery, and manifestation. With the tools and wisdom you have gained, you are now ready to step into your full power as a co-creator of your reality.

Remember: you are the creator of your destiny. The magic is within you.

XIV

Karm and the Collective Karm of Society

Introduction to Collective Karm: A Shared Web of Actions and Consequences

Karm, in its most personal form, is often seen as the law of cause and effect—a one-to-one connection between our actions and the outcomes we experience. However, there is another layer to this universal law that is often overlooked: the concept of collective karm. Just as individual actions create consequences, so too do the collective actions of societies, communities, and even entire nations.

Collective karm refers to the shared karmic energy that arises from the actions of groups of people. It suggests that the actions, thoughts, and decisions of a collective body—whether through governance, societal norms, or cultural practices—can shape the future for everyone involved, not just the individuals who directly participate in those actions.

This idea brings forth a compelling question: How do the actions of others—those we may not even know—affect our lives and our destinies? Is it possible for one person to bear the weight of another's karm? Can a child born into a polluted world, for example, be held responsible for the pollution created by previous generations? Or is that child merely carrying the consequences of others' actions?

Let us explore the deeper implications of this concept through a story that delves into the life of a young boy who must confront the collective karm of society.

Rudhav's Story: Born into the Legacy of Pollution

Rudhav's life began like that of many children—innocent, full of potential, and full of dreams. Born in the bustling city of Delhi, Rudhav's earliest years were marked by the usual milestones—learning to walk, to speak, to interact with the world around him. But unlike many children who grew up in cleaner environments, Rudhav's world was one of smog, dust, and the overwhelming stench of pollution.

From his first breath, Rudhav was surrounded by the harsh realities of a rapidly industrializing society. Delhi, like many major cities across the globe, had become an epicenter for environmental degradation, with its air quality consistently ranking among the worst in the world. What was once a place of vibrant culture and bustling streets was now a city struggling under the weight of unchecked industrial growth, overpopulation, and environmental neglect.

Rudhav's parents, both professionals, were well aware of the struggles that their city faced. But they had no choice. They had jobs in the city, and the family had to live where they could afford. Despite their awareness of the pollution, Rudhav's parents never thought that their child would be forced to bear the burden of the decisions made by previous generations. They didn't ask for the air to be this toxic, nor did they want their son to suffer the consequences of a world that had neglected its environmental responsibilities.

But as Rudhav grew, it became clear that the collective karm of society was catching up with him. At the age of five, he began to show signs of respiratory distress. Persistent coughs, wheezing, and shortness of breath were regular parts of his daily life. He was diagnosed with asthma, a disease that would become a constant companion throughout his childhood.

The doctor's diagnosis was grim: the toxic air Rudhav had breathed since birth had already begun to compromise his lungs. He had become part of a generation whose health was already at risk due to the environmental mistakes of others.

The Karm Behind Rudhav's Struggles: Understanding Collective Karm

At first glance, Rudhav's story may seem like a simple case of illness. It might appear that he was just unlucky, born in the wrong place at the wrong time. However, when we look deeper, we begin to see the workings of collective karm. Rudhav's suffering was not solely a result of his personal actions; it was the consequence of the actions of others—society at large, the industrial sectors, the governments, and even previous generations that had chosen growth over sustainability.

In this way, Rudhav's karm was interwoven with the karm of the world around him. He had no control over the decisions that led to the environmental crisis. He didn't choose to live in a city plagued by pollution, nor did he actively contribute to the decline of the air quality. Yet, because he was born into this reality, he was forced to endure its consequences.

This brings us to an important distinction in our understanding of karm: collective karm is not about individual choice, but about the shared consequences of actions taken by groups. Just as an individual's good or bad actions create karm for themself, the collective actions of society—such as overconsumption, negligence, and disregard for the environment—create a karmic legacy that affects everyone, even those who did not directly participate in those actions.

Rudhav's life became a reflection of the collective karm of a society that had placed short-term gain over long-term well-being. His suffering was not the result of his own personal misdeeds, but of the accumulated mistakes of those before him—the decisions made by people who prioritized industrial progress, economic development, and convenience over the health of the planet.

The Interconnectedness of Collective Karm

The story of Rudhav raises the question: if one person suffers due to the collective karm of society, what does this mean for the rest of us? Is it possible to change this shared karmic energy, or are we doomed to perpetuate the mistakes of the past?

The answer lies in the interconnectedness of all beings. Karm, whether individual or collective, is a reflection of how we interact with the world around us. Just as an individual's actions ripple out into the world, the actions of society, whether positive or negative, affect everyone within it. Rudhav's struggles with pollution are not isolated; they are part of a larger karmic web that includes not only his own life but the lives of all those affected by the choices of society.

However, the concept of collective karm also offers hope. Just as collective negative karm can create hardship and suffering, collective positive karm has the potential to bring healing and transformation. When individuals, communities, and societies come together with a shared sense of responsibility, they can shift the course of their collective karm.

For Rudhav, the solution lies not in his own actions alone, but in the actions of those around him. If society recognizes the consequences of its environmental actions and begins to take responsibility for healing the planet, it can begin to shift the karmic tide. This collective effort can lead to cleaner air, healthier lives, and a more sustainable future for all.

Reflection Exercises: Understanding Collective Karm in Your Life

To understand and address collective karm, it is important to examine how we, as individuals, contribute to the collective energy of society and the world. The following exercises are designed to help you explore your role in the collective karmic web and how you can contribute to positive change.

Exercise 1: Identifying Collective Actions

Objective: Recognize how the collective actions of society influence your life and the lives of others.

Instructions: Take some time to reflect on the actions of society that have impacted you or others around you. Consider the social, environmental, political, and economic decisions made by groups, organizations, and governments. How have these actions shaped your life, and how are they reflected in the challenges you face today?

Questions to Ponder:

1. How have I personally benefited from the collective actions of society (e.g., public health policies, education systems, etc.)?
2. What collective actions have negatively affected me or those around me (e.g., pollution, social injustice, economic inequality)?
3. How can I shift my own actions to positively contribute to the collective karm?

Activity: Write down three examples of collective karm you've personally encountered, whether positive or negative. Reflect on how they have affected your life and the lives of others.

Exercise 2: Shifting Collective Karm

Objective: Explore practical ways to contribute to positive collective karm through individual actions.

Instructions: Change begins with the individual, and each small action contributes to the larger whole. Reflect on areas where you can make a positive impact in your community or society at large. Whether it's through your choices in consumption, the way you treat others, or how you participate in environmental sustainability, your actions matter.

Questions to Ponder:

1. What are some small, everyday actions I can take to shift my personal karm toward a more positive direction?
2. How can I encourage my community to adopt more sustainable, compassionate, or socially responsible behaviors?
3. What societal changes would I like to see, and what role can I play in bringing them about?

Activity: Write a letter to your future self. In it, describe the changes you wish to see in society and your role in fostering those changes. Commit to three actions you will take over the next year to help shift the collective karm of your community or society.

Exercise 3: The Ripple Effect of Collective Karm

Objective: Understand the interconnectedness of all actions and how they affect the collective.

Instructions: The actions of individuals create a ripple effect that spreads out into the world. Spend some time reflecting on a recent decision you made and how it might have had consequences beyond just yourself.

Questions to Ponder:

1. How did my actions (even seemingly small ones) affect others around me, and what was the larger impact?

2. In what ways can my actions today create positive ripple effects for future generations?

Activity:

1. Think of a decision you made recently, whether at work, at home, or in your community. Reflect on its impact not just on you, but on others—locally, nationally, or even globally.
2. Write down the ripple effects of your actions and how they could contribute to either positive or negative collective karm. Make a plan to take conscious, positive actions moving forward.

Conclusion: Breaking the Cycle of Collective Karm

The story of Rudhav's life serves as a reminder that karm is not just an individual journey—it is a shared experience. The actions we take as individuals impact not only ourselves but also the broader web of society. And when we neglect our collective responsibilities, we create karmic consequences that can be felt for generations.

However, just as the actions of the past have shaped the present, the actions we take today can shape the future. By acknowledging the weight of collective karm and working together to create a more just, compassionate, and sustainable world, we can begin to heal the wounds created by past mistakes. The future, after all, is not written in stone—it is shaped by the choices we make today, both as individuals and as a collective.

XV

Living a Karmically Aligned Life: Daily Practices for Transformation

Living a karmically aligned life is more than just understanding the concept of Karm—it's about integrating its teachings into our daily actions, thoughts, and relationships. It's about living in a way that aligns with the universal principles of balance, truth, and compassion. This chapter will explore practical ways you can live a karmically aligned life, focusing on daily practices that encourage personal growth, harmony with others, and a deeper connection to your inner self.

Understanding Karmic Alignment

To live karmically aligned means to act with conscious awareness and intention, understanding that every thought, word, and deed ripples out into the world and returns to you. It means living with a sense of purpose that is in harmony with your highest values and the natural order of life. Every decision you make contributes to the creation of your karmic journey, shaping the life you lead and the experiences you attract.

Karm, in this sense, is not just about "good" or "bad" actions. It's a system of energy flow and consequences. The energy you put into the world through your actions, intentions, and attitudes is the energy that will return to you, often in unexpected ways. Thus, living karmically aligned is about being aware of the energy you are generating and consciously choosing how you contribute to the world.

Why Is Karmic Alignment Important?

Living in alignment with your karmic path brings several benefits:

Inner Peace: When you live in harmony with universal principles, you experience a sense of peace that comes from knowing your actions are aligned with your higher purpose.

Personal Growth: Aligning with Karm helps you learn from your experiences. Each action is an opportunity to grow and evolve spiritually and emotionally.

Harmonious Relationships: By being aware of how your actions affect others, you build better, more authentic relationships based on mutual respect and understanding.

Manifestation of Abundance: When your actions are in line with the flow of universal energy, you open the door to attracting greater prosperity, success, and opportunities.

Healing: As you make conscious, aligned choices, you begin to heal old wounds—whether from past karmic patterns or from trauma—and create space for new, more positive experiences.

The Role of Daily Practices in Karmic Alignment

The key to living a karmically aligned life is daily practice. It's through consistent, mindful actions that we gradually align our lives with higher principles. Here are some practical, transformative practices to help you live in alignment with Karm:

1. Practice Mindfulness: Be Aware of Your Thoughts and Actions

Mindfulness is a foundational practice for karmic alignment. It involves being present in every moment and fully aware of your thoughts, feelings, and actions. This awareness allows you to observe when you are acting out of alignment with your true self or karmic purpose.

How to practice mindfulness:

1. Start each day with a few minutes of deep breathing or meditation. Focus on the present moment and clear your mind of distractions.
2. Throughout the day, pause regularly to check in with yourself. Ask, "Am I acting with integrity? Am I being mindful of my actions, and do they align with my higher self?"
3. Practice mindful communication by listening fully when others speak and speaking with kindness, honesty, and compassion.

4. Pay attention to your emotions and thoughts, especially when faced with challenges. Notice if your reactions are based on fear, ego, or old patterns, and choose to respond from a place of wisdom.

2. Cultivate Compassion and Empathy: Treat Others as You Wish to Be Treated

One of the core tenets of karmic alignment is recognizing the interconnectedness of all beings. What you do to others, you do to yourself. Compassion and empathy are essential practices for generating positive Karm. By treating others with love, understanding, and kindness, you not only improve their lives but also create positive energy that will return to you.

How to cultivate compassion and empathy?

1. Practice random acts of kindness. Whether it's helping someone in need, offering a compliment, or simply being present for someone who is struggling, small acts of kindness can shift your energy and positively impact others.
2. Spend time in nature or in quiet contemplation to develop a sense of connection with the world around you. This helps you develop compassion for all living beings.
3. When interacting with others, especially those who challenge you, try to see the situation from their perspective. Responding with empathy and understanding can diffuse tension and create positive energy.

3. Take Responsibility for Your Actions: Own Your Karmic Energy

Taking responsibility for your actions, thoughts, and words is crucial to living karmically aligned. It's easy to blame others or external circumstances for the challenges we face, but true transformation comes from owning your role in every experience.

How to take responsibility?

1. Reflect regularly on your actions. If something doesn't go as planned or you hurt someone, take time to understand how your actions contributed to the situation.
2. Practice self-forgiveness. If you've made mistakes, acknowledge them, learn from them, and let go of guilt. Holding onto negative energy only creates more karmic baggage.
3. When faced with difficult situations or challenges, ask yourself: "What can I learn from this? How can I use this experience to grow and evolve?"

4. Set Intentions Aligned with Your Higher Self: Create Positive Karmic Ripples

The intentions behind your actions are just as important as the actions themselves. Setting positive, clear intentions is a way of consciously choosing to align with your higher self, rather than being swayed by external circumstances or ego-driven desires.

How to set aligned intentions?

1. Begin each day with a positive affirmation or intention. For example: "Today, I will act with kindness and integrity in all that I do."
2. Before making decisions, especially major ones, ask yourself: "Is this aligned with my true purpose? Will this

choice bring me closer to my authentic self?"

3. Reflect on your intentions regularly. Are they based on love, service, and compassion? Or are they driven by fear, ego, or the need for validation? Adjust your intentions as needed to stay in alignment with your highest self.

5. Let Go of Attachment: Trust the Flow of the Universe

Karmically aligned living requires the ability to let go of attachment. This doesn't mean giving up your desires or goals; it means releasing the need to control every outcome and trusting that the universe has a plan for you. When you release attachment, you free yourself from the burden of expectations, which allows for the natural flow of positive energy into your life.

How to practice letting go?

1. Recognize when you are becoming attached to outcomes. If you're obsessing over a specific result, take a step back and remind yourself that everything is unfolding as it should.
2. Practice the art of surrender. Trust that the universe is always guiding you, even if things don't unfold as you expect.
3. Meditate on the concept of non-attachment. Reflect on how your attachment to material success, approval, or perfection can create karmic blockages and stress in your life.

6. Embrace Self-Love: Heal Your Past Karmic Wounds

Self-love is one of the most powerful ways to transform your karmic patterns. When you love and accept yourself, you stop projecting your insecurities, fears, and unresolved emotional baggage onto others. Self-love helps you heal old wounds and creates a foundation of inner peace from which all other positive actions flow.

How to practice self-love?

1. Start by acknowledging your worth. Every day, remind yourself that you are deserving of love, happiness, and peace.
2. Engage in activities that nurture your body, mind, and soul—whether it's yoga, journaling, or spending time with loved ones.
3. Forgive yourself for past mistakes. Understand that you are not defined by your past actions and that every day is a new opportunity to make better choices.
4. Set boundaries that protect your energy and preserve your peace of mind. Saying no when necessary is a powerful form of self-care.

7. Practice Gratitude: Shift Your Energy

Gratitude is a powerful karmic tool. It shifts your focus from lack to abundance, from negativity to positivity. By regularly practicing gratitude, you align your energy with the universe's flow of abundance, and this positive energy ripples outward to create more of the same.

How to practice gratitude?

1. Keep a gratitude journal. Every day, write down three things you are grateful for.
2. Practice gratitude in the moment. When something good happens, take a moment to feel gratitude and appreciation, no matter how small the gesture or outcome.

3. Cultivate a grateful mindset. Try to find something to appreciate in every situation, even in difficult times. Gratitude transforms challenges into opportunities for growth.

Conclusion: Creating Your Karmic Path

Living a karmically aligned life is a continuous journey of self-awareness, transformation, and conscious action. By integrating daily practices that encourage mindfulness, compassion, self-love, and responsible action, you begin to shape your life into one that is in harmony with your higher self and the universe.

Karmic alignment doesn't happen overnight, but with consistent effort and intention, you will start to notice the shifts in your life. Your relationships will improve, your inner peace will grow, and the energy you send into the world will come back to you in ways you cannot yet imagine. Remember, every moment is an opportunity to realign, reset, and create the life you are meant to live.

Reflection Exercises:

1. **Mindfulness Check-In:** Throughout your day, pause at least three times to check in with your thoughts and actions. Are they aligned with your values? How can you redirect your energy to be more aligned with your true self?
2. **Gratitude Journal:** Each night, write down at least five things you are grateful for. Observe how this practice shifts your mindset and energy.

3. **Intentions Reflection:** At the beginning of each week, set three intentions that align with your higher purpose. At the end of the week, reflect on how your actions and experiences connected with these intentions.
4. **Self-Love Practice:** Dedicate 15 minutes each day to nurturing yourself—whether through a relaxing bath, reading, meditation, or simply sitting in quiet reflection.

How does this practice impact your sense of well-being and peace?

These practices, when implemented with intention, will gradually guide you toward a more karmically aligned and transformative life.

XVI

Karmic Healing Through Art and Creativity: A Holistic Approach to Transformation

Introduction

Art and creativity have long been considered powerful tools for healing and personal transformation. Whether through painting, music, writing, dance, or any other form of creative expression, the act of creation has the potential to heal emotional wounds, shift energetic blockages, and facilitate karmic transformation. When we understand the deeper connection between art and karma, we see that creativity isn't just about self-expression—it's a direct path to karmic healing.

This chapter blends key concepts from previous chapters in the book, such as Karmic Alignment, Dharmic Purpose, and Meditation, into the practice of art and creativity. Through this integrated approach, we can create a life that is aligned with our true purpose, release negative karmic patterns, and actively rewrite our destiny through the transformative power of creative expression.

The Role of Karma in Art and Creativity

At the heart of every artistic expression lies the individual's intention. The karmic law of cause and effect teaches us that every thought, word, and deed generates an energetic imprint that reverberates through time. Our actions—both creative and destructive—leave karmic footprints that can either lead us toward greater spiritual growth or keep us locked in cycles of suffering.

When it comes to artistic expression, this principle rings true. For example, consider a piece of music. The composer channels their emotions, thoughts, and experiences into the creation. Whether these emotions are rooted in love, anger, joy, or pain, the energy of the composer is embedded in the music itself. Listeners who engage with the music receive the energy from the artist, whether consciously or unconsciously, and the karmic cycle continues.

In a similar vein, karmic healing through art involves creating or engaging with art as a way to clear past karmic imprints and re-align with our higher dharmic purpose. Artistic practices allow us to explore and express the energy of our inner world, illuminating unconscious thoughts, beliefs, and patterns that may be blocking our growth.

When these patterns are revealed, they can be healed through the very act of creation, breaking cycles of negative karma and realigning us with a path of peace and purpose.

Art as a Mirror: Recognizing and Understanding Karmic Imprints

As discussed in Chapter 1, the concept of Karmic Awareness is crucial to transforming our karma. The first step in karmic healing through art is recognizing the karmic imprints that have shaped our lives. This awareness can be achieved by using art as a mirror—a reflection of our inner state.

When we create or engage with art, we access the subconscious, where past karmic experiences are often stored. For instance, if you feel compelled to paint an image of a person or place from your past, or if a song evokes strong emotional reactions, these responses often signal unresolved karma. Art brings these imprints to the surface, allowing us to confront and examine them without judgment. This process of self-reflection through creative expression facilitates the release of negative patterns that may have been holding us back.

Exercise: Recognizing Karmic Patterns Through Art

Take a moment to reflect on a significant moment from your past that still holds emotional weight. Using your preferred medium—whether it's painting, drawing, or writing—create a representation of that memory. As you engage in the process, notice any emotions that surface. What beliefs or patterns are associated with this event? Are there recurring themes in your life that need to be addressed? Document your insights and explore how these patterns might be playing out in your current life.

Art for Release: Letting Go of Negative Karma

Healing karma involves the release of negative emotional energy that binds us to past experiences. In Chapter 3: Breaking the Cycle of Karma, we discussed how karma isn't just about past actions—it's also about the accumulated emotional and energetic imprints from past lives or early life experiences. Art allows us to create a safe space to release this emotional energy, enabling the karmic cycle to be broken.

When we release through art, we are no longer bound by the past but free to create a new, more positive future. Creative expression provides an outlet for repressed emotions, unresolved trauma, and lingering negative thoughts. As we allow ourselves to feel and express these emotions through art, we experience catharsis—a release of the energy tied to past experiences, which helps to clear our karmic debt.

Exercise: Releasing Negative Karmic Imprints Through Creative Expression

Choose an experience from your past that continues to influence your life negatively. Create an artwork that symbolizes the release of this energy. If you're painting, allow your brushstrokes to reflect the emotional weight of the experience. If you're writing, allow the words to flow freely, expressing your frustrations, anger, or sadness. Once the piece is complete, reflect on how you feel. Is there a sense of release or lightness? If possible, consider safely destroying the piece (burning, tearing, or dissolving it), symbolizing the final release of that karmic energy.

Rewriting Your Destiny: Karmic Transformation through Art

In Chapter 3: Breaking the Cycle of Karm, we explored the idea that it's not enough to simply release negative karma—we must actively work to create new, positive karmic imprints. Art provides a powerful medium for rewriting the stories we tell ourselves and the energy we bring into the world. Through creative practices, we can reframe our experiences, heal past wounds, and manifest new realities aligned with our highest purpose.

Just as the law of attraction teaches us to focus on what we wish to create, the act of creating art allows us to visualize and materialize our desired reality. Art helps us embody new identities, explore possibilities, and manifest positive change.

Exercise: Creative Manifestation of New Karmic Patterns

Create a vision board or a piece of art that represents the future you wish to create. Use symbolism, colors, and images that embody your dreams, goals, and values. As you create, immerse yourself in the emotion of living this new life—feel the excitement, the joy, the peace that comes with aligning your actions with your dharmic purpose. Keep this artwork in a place where you can regularly view it, as a constant reminder of the positive changes you are manifesting.

Art as Meditation: The Mind-Body Connection in Karmic Healing

In Chapter 10: Meditation and Mindfulness, we discussed how the present moment is the gateway to karmic healing. Meditation allows us to connect to our higher self and experience clarity and peace. The act of creating art can be a form of meditation, a way to access the flow state where we are deeply connected to our intuition and the present moment.

When we create art with mindfulness and intention, we enter a meditative state that calms the mind, balances the body, and heals the spirit. The energy from this creative process can break the chains of past karma, reprogramming the unconscious mind and leading to the manifestation of new, more harmonious experiences.

Exercise: Mindful Art Creation

Set aside time for a mindful art session where your only goal is to be fully present. Whether you choose to paint, draw, or engage in any other creative practice, focus on each step of the process. Notice the brushstrokes, the flow of the colors, or the texture of the materials. Let go of any judgment about the end result, and simply immerse yourself in the act of creation. Allow this process to calm your mind and center your energy in the present moment.

Art as Dharmic Expression: Aligning Creativity with Purpose

As we explored in Chapter 5: Dharm, Karm, and Goals, dharma is the path of right living—aligning our actions with our higher purpose. Art becomes a powerful tool for dharmic expression when it is created with the intention of serving both the self and the greater good. Just as we align our daily actions with dharma, we can align our creative practices with our highest truth, using art to express our soul's purpose and contribute to the collective healing of the world.

Creating with dharmic intention ensures that our creative work contributes to positive karmic energy, not just for ourselves but for others as well. When we create with awareness, focusing on love, healing, and service, we generate powerful, life-affirming energy that ripples out into the world.

Exercise: Art for Higher Purpose

Create a piece of artwork with the specific intention of healing, uplifting, or serving others. This could be through making art for someone in need, creating a public mural or installation, or designing a project that promotes social justice or spiritual growth. As you create, focus on the intention to bring healing, joy, and peace to those who experience your work.

Conclusion

Transforming Karma through Creativity

Art and creativity are transformative forces that allow us to engage deeply with our karmic journey. By using art as a tool for self-awareness, release, and transformation, we can heal past wounds, clear negative patterns, and align ourselves with our true dharmic path. Creativity is not just a means of self-expression—it is a profound spiritual practice that helps us rewrite our karmic story, one brushstroke, note, or word at a time.

By integrating the principles of mindfulness, dharmic purpose, and karmic awareness into our artistic practices, we unlock the potential for profound healing and transformation. As we create with intention and awareness, we not only heal ourselves but contribute to the collective karmic healing of the world, creating a ripple effect of love, peace, and positive transformation.

Karmic Healing Through Art: Exercises

Karmic Reflection Through Art:
Take a piece of art you've created in the past (or create a new piece), and reflect on the emotions and karmic themes that arose during its creation. What does the piece reveal about your past karmic patterns? Write about your insights.

Manifesting Positive Karma:
Spend time reflecting on a positive goal or intention you wish to manifest. Create a vision board or artwork that represents this intention, and display it somewhere you can see it daily. As you gaze at it, remind yourself that every act of creation plants seeds of positive karma.

Group Art for Collective Healing:
Collaborate with others to create an artwork that represents a collective intention for global healing. This could be a community mural, a charity art event, or even a shared poem or song that speaks to unity and love. Reflect on how your combined creative energy can uplift the collective consciousness.

XVII

The Divine Play of Karm: Understanding the Bigger Picture

Introduction

The universe, as described in ancient spiritual philosophies, particularly in Hinduism and Buddhism, is not merely a physical reality—it is a divine play (Lila) orchestrated by the Divine. Just as an artist weaves a masterpiece with infinite detail, the Divine weaves the fabric of existence, where every action is part of a grand design. Karm, as the energy that arises from every being's consciousness, plays a crucial role in this dance. Every thought, word, and deed is a movement in this cosmic drama.

Karm is never isolated; it is part of an interdependent system. The energy of our actions reverberates through the collective, connecting us to everyone and everything. This understanding helps us see that we are not isolated beings, but interconnected souls playing unique roles in a grand cosmic narrative. Recognizing this interconnectedness shifts us from a mindset of separateness to one of collective responsibility, where our actions affect not just ourselves but the entire collective experience.

The Road Ahead: The Divine Union of Karm and Destiny

The teachings in this book have laid the foundation for your transformation, but this is just the beginning of your spiritual journey. The process of self-discovery and spiritual growth is ongoing, and as you continue on this path, you will explore deeper dimensions of consciousness, experience profound shifts in awareness, and uncover more of the mysteries that the universe holds for you.

As we look ahead, we will delve into advanced spiritual practices and concepts that will further accelerate your evolution, helping you step into your full potential as a co-creator of your reality. In the next edition, we will explore:

Advanced Meditation Practices: Beyond mindfulness, we will explore techniques that will unlock deeper states of consciousness, enabling you to access higher dimensions of awareness, connect with your higher self, and cultivate lasting inner peace.

The Science of Manifestation: Manifestation is grounded in the principles of quantum physics and energy. We will uncover how to work with the energetic field to manifest at will, tapping into the invisible forces that shape our reality.

Karmic Relationships: Relationships are often the most complex aspects of our lives, and within them lie powerful lessons for growth. We will dive into the dynamics of karmic relationships, teaching you how to navigate them with conscious awareness, compassion, and spiritual maturity.

Living in Alignment with Your Soul's Purpose: Your journey is about stepping into the highest version of yourself, fine-tuning your life's path, and aligning with your soul's true desires. We will explore how to live a life of grace, purpose, and fulfillment, manifesting your true destiny with joy and ease.

The Climax: The Divine Union of Karm and Destiny

The true climax of your spiritual journey is the realization that you are both the creator and the experiencer of your reality. This is when you begin to understand that Karm, the law of cause and effect, is not just a system of rewards and punishments but a divine play—a cosmic dance that involves every being, every action, and every event within the universe. It is in this dance that you realize you are not a victim of your circumstances but the master of your fate.

When you grasp this, the magic of life begins to unfold. You are no longer bound by limiting beliefs or karmic patterns of the past. Instead, you can manifest your highest potential effortlessly. The energy of love, peace, and abundance will flow through you, guiding you toward your deepest desires and dreams.

This process of spiritual evolution is not just about personal success or material achievement. It is about returning to your true nature—an eternal, limitless being in perfect harmony with the universe. When you understand that you are not separate from the universe, but an integral part of it, life becomes a continuous dance of creation, where every thought, word, and action is an expression of your divine essence.

Understanding Karmic Debt and Reincarnation

The larger cycle of Karm, encompassing multiple lifetimes, offers a broader perspective. Each life is a stage in the soul's evolution, and the challenges we face are opportunities for growth that may have been set into motion by our actions in past lives. This understanding of Karmic debt helps us approach life's difficulties with patience, knowing they are not random but opportunities for healing and evolution.

When we act from ego, seeking control, validation, or personal gain, we create non-spontaneous Karm, binding ourselves to cycles of desire and attachment. But the divine play of Karm invites us to let go of our illusions of control and surrender to the flow of life. By releasing the ego and trusting in the greater plan, we enter the cosmic dance, where our actions are in harmony with the unfolding of the universe.

Dharm: The Guiding Force in the Divine Play

Dharm, the righteous path or purpose that aligns us with our higher self, plays a vital role in the divine play of Karm. When we act in accordance with our Dharm, we align ourselves with the cosmic flow of Karm, playing our part in the greater drama of existence. This alignment allows us to rise above the limitations of the ego, viewing challenges not as burdens but as opportunities to act with purpose, compassion, and grace.

Compassion: The Key to Transcending Karm

The divine play of Karm teaches us the importance of compassion. Compassion binds all beings together and ensures the harmonious flow of Karm. As we move through life's challenges, we are called to act with compassion—not just towards others but also towards ourselves. Compassion becomes the key to transcending past wounds and clearing negative Karmic patterns. By cultivating compassion, we release judgment, forgive past wrongs, and open ourselves to the healing energy of the universe.

The Bigger Picture: Letting Go of Attachment

The divine play of Karm reminds us that we are not the center of the universe. We are but one part of a much larger design. When we release our attachment to outcomes and embrace the unfolding of life with trust and faith, we can align ourselves with the greater flow of the cosmic dance.

When we act in alignment with our Dharm, surrender the ego, and embrace compassion, we move through life with grace and ease, knowing that each moment is part of the divine play—a play where we are both actors and spectators. In this divine drama, we are called not just to act, but to act with awareness, purpose, and love, contributing our energy to the cosmic dance that shapes the universe.

Conclusion

Living in Harmony with the Divine Play of Karm

As you close this chapter, know that the journey is far from over. You have only just begun to tap into the incredible potential within you. The path ahead will be filled with endless opportunities for growth, discovery, and manifestation. With the tools and wisdom you have gained, you are now ready to step into your full power as a co-creator of your reality.

Remember: You are the creator of your destiny. The magic is within you.

TRAILER FOR THE NEXT EDITION:

"The Path to Spiritual Mastery: Unlocking the Secrets of the Universe"

In the next edition, we'll go even deeper into the mysteries of spiritual mastery. What if you could manifest effortlessly? What if you could heal all of your past karm in an instant? What if you could step into your destiny and live a life beyond your wildest dreams?

This is not a fantasy. It is your divine birth right. In the upcoming volume, you'll learn:

- How to dissolve the illusion of separation and step into your true power.
- The secrets of timeless meditation techniques that will guide you into higher dimensions of consciousness.
- The hidden dynamics of karmic patterns and how to transform them quickly and effortlessly.
- How to master the energetic laws of manifestation to bring anything you desire into your reality with ease.

Prepare yourself to step into a new era of your life. The journey of spiritual mastery is waiting. Are you ready to claim your true power and unlock the secrets of the universe?

Final Thoughts: A New Beginning

As you close this book, remember that this is not the end but a new beginning. You are now equipped with the tools and the wisdom to transform your life in profound and miraculous ways. Your journey is unique, and your potential is limitless.

Trust the process. Trust yourself. You are the architect of your reality. The universe is your canvas.

Embrace the power of karm and manifestation, and step boldly into your divine destiny.

Thank you for taking this journey with me. Until we meet again in the next edition—may your path be filled with love, light, and infinite blessings.

www.ingramcontent.com/pod-product-compliance
Lightning Source LLC
LaVergne TN
LVHW041102150826
845673LV00007B/1892

9798896326946